IN THE FIELD

IN THE FIELD

Readings on the Field Research Experience,
SECOND EDITION

Edited by
Carolyn D. Smith and William Kornblum

Westport, Connecticut
London

Library of Congress Cataloging-in-Publication Data

In the field : readings on the field research experience / edited by
  Carolyn D. Smith and William Kornblum. — 2nd ed.
      p.   cm.
    Includes bibliographical references and index.
    ISBN 0-275-95416-1 (alk. paper). — ISBN 0-275-95417-X (pbk. :
  alk. paper)
    1. Ethnology—Field work.   2. Participant observation.   3. Social
  sciences—Field work.   I. Smith, Carolyn D.   II. Kornblum, William.
  GN346.I5   1996
  306'.072—dc20   96-10431

British Library Cataloguing in Publication Data is available.

Library of Congress Catalog Card Number: 96-10431
ISBN: 0-275-95416-1
ISBN: 0-275-95417-X (pbk.)

First published in 1996

Praeger Publishers, 88 Post Road West, Westport, CT 06881
An imprint of Greenwood Publishing Group, Inc.

Printed in the United States of America

The paper used in this book complies with the
Permanent Paper Standard issued by the National
Information Standards Organization (Z39.48-1984).

10 9 8 7 6 5 4 3 2 1

Contents

PART III: MAINTAINING OBJECTIVITY

PART IV: THE OBSERVER'S ROLE

EPILOGUE

Preface

Social scientists who engage in ethnographic field research often become deeply involved in the lives of the people they are studying. In some cases the researcher actually becomes a member of the group or community and participates fully in its day-to-day activities. This experience can have a profound effect on the researcher, who often must reexamine his or her values and attitudes and may be forced to make choices that would not be required in the ordinary course of events. This collection of readings from ethnographic researchers' personal accounts is intended to give students and other readers a taste of what it is really like to conduct research "in the field."

The selections in this book do not focus on methodology, although all of the contributors to this volume are known for their ethnographic research skills. Moreover, while they all believe in the value of this research method, they understand its limitations and recognize that it could not exist independently of other approaches. Yet to varying degrees their experiences in the field have shaped their subsequent research endeavors and, often, their outlook on life.

This volume presents a set of personal accounts by practicing field researchers. It is about how they do their research and how they feel while they are doing it. The authors describe how they became accepted by the people they wished to know, how they built and maintained relationships with their subjects, how they worked to maintain their objectivity as researchers, and how they sorted through their research findings and worried about the privacy of the friends they had made in the field.

The editors would like to take this opportunity to thank all of the contributors to this volume for their generous support and cooperation.

Introduction

WILLIAM KORNBLUM

When night fell the family gathered around the campfire, and when the early part of the evening passed without incident, the young adults drifted beyond the limits of the fire. The older Boyash [gypsies] continued to trade stories over the remaining wine and coffee. Then, just as they were dispersing, a small hail of stones landed around the main courtyard of the camp.

Within seconds the family was readying itself for bloody battle. Most of those who had lingered around the fire were women and, incensed at the resumption of hostilities, they ran from wagon to wagon summoning the men and gathering all available weapons. I had retired to my *roulotte* [wagon] and was about to undress for bed when Persa burst into the wagon. She shouted that the Serbians were throwing stones again; we were going out to stop them. I would have hesitated, flattered that the family felt so comfortable with me that they would ask me to fight on their behalf. I was also worried about getting hurt. But Persa had no sympathy for the distinction between participant and observer. She thrust a heavy stick in my hand and shoved me toward the door.

As I found my way to the main road through the camp, my worst fears were confirmed. It seemed there would be a pitched battle, for the Boyash men and women were grouped about 50 yards away from a much larger group of Serbian men. Both groups were heavily armed. I saw Cortez flick open his switchblade. Tony was holding a shotgun. The Boyash women kept up a steady barrage of violent oaths and insults. As we slowly advanced toward the Serbians I attempted to find a place in the second ranks, but Persa was there again to shove me to the front.

This is an excerpt from the field notes I wrote during a research sojourn with Boyash gypsies in a shantytown on the outskirts of Paris. It describes a dispute between "my" family of gypsies and a nearby encampment of Serbian immigrants. For the family with whom I was living at the time, the importance of the incident lay in the fact that they had demonstrated their willingness to defend their honor, using violence if necessary. For me, a foreign ethnographer and participant observer, it was significant because despite my ambivalence and fear I had stood with "my" people in the face of danger. In a moment of crisis I had become one of them.

Ethnographic research is not always this exciting or dangerous. The ethnographer's goal is to describe the way of life of a particular group from within, that is, by understanding and communicating not only what happens but how the members of the group interpret and understand what happens. The primary technique used in ethnographic research is participant observation, which usually involves living or otherwise spending extended periods with the people one is trying to understand.

Usually the most trying aspect of this kind of research is the effort to obtain permission to spend time with the people one wishes to get to know. Once this is accomplished (and it is never entirely achieved), the work of observation and description can become, on the surface, quite routine and even boring. One is there day after day, watching and gently asking questions. At times the questions are annoying; one's very presence may become a drag. From the standpoint of those being observed, the observer is ignorant of the most obvious truths and constantly exposes that ignorance by questioning behavior that everyone else takes for granted. In short, our respondents often find us tiresome unless we have something to offer them other than just our goodwill. Thus, it occurred to Persa that my size would be an asset to the gypsies, so she pushed me to the front line.

Persa and I never discussed that incident (which, happily, was resolved without actual violence), but I could tell that it had changed her opinion of me from one of disdain to one of guarded respect. It is rare for the subjects of ethnographic research to go on record about their feelings regarding the research, but the novelist Ken Kesey offered an insightful metaphor in a speech he gave some years ago. Best known for his gripping but fictional account of life in a mental hospital, *One Flew Over the Cuckoo's Nest*, Kesey himself was the subject of a quasi-ethnographic study: He and his circle of hippie friends, known as the Merry Pranksters, were described by Tom Wolfe in *The Electric Kool-Aid Acid Test*. In the 1960s Wolfe was just beginning his career as an ethnographic journalist, yet he was already renowned for his steadfast uninvolvement in the lives of his subjects, as well as for his cool white linen suits. One day he was sitting with the Merry Pranksters in a room of Kesey's house while Kesey was painting the ceiling. A glob of yellow paint fell on the observer's immaculate white jacket, and although Wolfe wiped off the paint with studied calmness, he was unable to hide his profound annoyance. "That's how it is, Tom," said Kesey. "If you want to get down in it you've got to get some of it on you."

This comment goes to the heart of the participant observer's dilemma: To what extent does one become involved in and participate in the lives of the people one is observing? All social-scientific ethnographers, and many journalists like Tom Wolfe, experience some version of this dilemma. I experienced it in the incident described earlier, and I have encountered it in one form or another in every field research study I have engaged in. Nor does the researcher have much control over how the dilemma of participation versus observation will present itself. For Douglas Harper, the issue was raised immediately as he learned how to survive as a tramp. For Claire Sterk, too, the issue was raised quite soon after she began spending time with prostitutes on the stroll. For William F. Whyte, the dilemma was present as he befriended the Martini family and became accepted in the community, but it manifested itself most strongly later in his study, when he was asked to work in a local election campaign and found that he was expected to break the law by voting more than once for the same candidate.

Of all the methods employed in modern social science, ethnographic field research requires the most intense involvement with one's subjects. The ethnographer's "presentation of self" and the changes he or she experiences are part of the research process itself. These aspects of the method enrich the data gathered in this way by adding personal and emotional depth, but they also lead to endless complications, as many of the selections in this volume will show.

Those of us who practice the techniques of ethnographic research often write about our experiences as participant observers as well as other aspects of the ethnographic craft. However, our accounts of what we actually do in the field and the adventures we encounter there are usually buried in "methodological appendixes" to our published works. Other people, not ourselves, are the subjects of our research; when we speak of our own experiences in the field, we often do so only as an afterthought. Yet quite frequently these understated accounts of personal fieldwork experiences contain episodes or images that become widely known in their own right. An example is Whyte's famous account of how he came to know "Doc" in *Street Corner Society*. In this case, and in many others as well, the writer's descriptions of his own field research experiences are valuable statements about the nature of ethnographic research.

In recent years the writings of ethnographers have come under a great deal of scrutiny and criticism.[1] One point that has emerged from this evaluation is that modern ethnographies are less likely to follow a standard format than were earlier works of this type. Current ethnographies reflect more of the writers' literary and social-scientific sensibilities than did earlier studies, which followed a well-known analytical outline. The generality of this trend and its implications are surely worthy of attention. The authors represented in this volume, however, reflect on the interpersonal qualities of the ethnographic experience itself. By and large, they are writing about emotional and other issues associated with this research style, rather than about the equally vexing problems of meaning and communication.

It is also worth noting that ethnographic field research is a method in which one person typically gathers and analyzes the data. Reliance on individual effort is somewhat uncommon in this age of larger-scale and more bureaucratic research programs, which employ numerous research assistants and co-principal investigators. However, even when the ethnographer is employed with others in a larger study—as is often the case with AIDS or drug research of large-scale policy evaluations—it remains true that the observer often works alone, equipped with little more than a notebook and a pen (and at times a tape recorder or a camera). This was certainly true for each of the authors included here. Yet many of them had the support of larger organizations that encouraged their efforts and helped sustain them. Sterk's research was funded and supervised by the U.S. Centers for Disease Control in Atlanta and by an agency of the New York State Division of Substance Abuse Studies. Her field notes and much of the data she collected were often used by other researchers for different purposes. This is also true of the research conducted by Terry Williams, Edmundo Morales, and, to a somewhat lesser extent, Ruth Horowitz and me. Our books are about what we saw and experienced as individuals, but our research was part of a larger enterprise and might not have been possible otherwise. In sum, although ethnography is always a solo enterprise, increasingly the researcher needs the support of other professionals.

*   *   *

Whether they are working alone or as part of a larger research team, the relationships that develop between ethnographic researchers and the people they are studying are critical to the success of their research. Certain key aspects of those relationships serve as the basis for the organization of this book. Part I, "Gaining Entry," deals with the confusing and frustrating period every field researcher goes through while trying to gain acceptance by the people under study. Thus, Elijah Anderson writes about the custom of "going for cousins" (using a fictive kinship term to signify close friendship), which resulted in sponsorship for him as he undertook his research among black men in a low-income neighborhood on Chicago's South Side. (A researcher who has a "sponsor" has the support of a well-known, highly credible member of the community under study.) Carol Stack gained the trust of the women in The Flats largely by being helpful and sympathetic—providing daily assistance with the children or the shopping, listening to complaints about the welfare office, and the like. For Terry Williams the problem was more complex. When a researcher is observing illegal activities, the normal difficulties of gaining entry are compounded by the greater risk respondents run in taking the researcher into their confidence. The researcher also has to find a way of not participating in the illegal activity while still gaining the acceptance of those who are participating in it. In his essay on cocaine use in illegal after-hours clubs in New York City, Williams stresses the importance of outward symbols like dress in gaining acceptance, and explains how he managed to observe cocaine users without using the drug himself.

Peggy Sullivan and Kirk Elifson faced a somewhat different problem in their study of a religious sect whose worship services include serpent handling. While the activity is not illegal, it is often considered deviant, causing the participants to view outsiders with suspicion. In their chapter, "In the Field with Snake Handlers," Sullivan and Elifson describe how they gained the confidence of the group's members and were given permission to conduct their research.

Part II, "Building Relationships," continues with the theme of gaining the confidence of respondents; it shows how ethnographic researchers often develop subtle, complex relationships with some of their informants. Robert McNamara, Ruth Horowitz, and Douglas Harper all had to work hard to build and maintain relationships with their subjects. These selections also illustrate the impact of differences in race, gender, and class between the researcher and his or her subjects. McNamara describes how he had to pass a series of "tests" before he could be trusted by male hustlers in New York City's Times Square area. Horowitz, a white woman among male Chicano gang members, and Harper, a representative of the "respectable" world traveling with Carl, a tramp, also had to deal with the disparity between their backgrounds and those of their subjects. As Harper put it, "I never really learned to experience the world as a tramp and I knew that unless I moved completely into that life my values would probably remain in the world of relationships and commitments."

Despite such differences, field researchers persist, continually trying to find ways of reciprocating and empathizing with their subjects. But as illustrated in Part III, "Maintaining Objectivity," empathy itself can become a problem. How do ethnographic researchers deal with the need to be objective, to describe life the way they see it without glossing over unfavorable aspects because of their emotional involvement with the people they are studying? The researcher must not let friendships get in the way of his or her critical faculties. Related to this issue is the question of how deeply to become involved in the lives of the people one is studying. Whyte encountered this problem in the case of repeat voting mentioned earlier, as well as in his participation in community sports—on one occasion he made the game-winning hit in a neighborhood baseball game.

Claire Sterk and Victor Ayala obviously could not participate in the day-to-day life of the prostitutes, drug users, and homeless people they were observing, but over many months of close observation they were greatly affected by the impact of AIDS on these groups; the mounting death rate and accompanying hopelessness almost caused them to abandon their research. In my own case, the issue of objectivity is illustrated by the episode in which I went out of my way to receive a tongue-lashing from a steel company boss in order to see for myself how he treated employees. One does not ordinarily seek out such an experience, but if I had avoided the incident as my fellow workers recommended, I would have been acting according to their values rather than those of an objective researcher.

Part IV, "The Observer's Role," addresses a special problem of the participant observer. Not only must the observer maintain objectivity, he or she must arrive at some conclusion about the morality of observing other people. In this section, therefore, the researchers step back a little and ask some searching questions about observation itself. Edmundo Morales and Charles Bosk have observed and written about questionable behaviors. Each has wondered about his right to observe those behaviors, and each has attempted to resolve this issue, although it is not one for which there are any easy solutions. In the final selection, Nancy Naples describes the problems she encountered as an urban outsider in a world of rural women. Her experience led her to better understand the advantages and disadvantages for the ethnographer of being an "outsider" in a world of "insiders."

The book ends with an epilogue that is both a beginning and an ending. Like many other social-scientific researchers, Vernon Boggs had a passionate interest that he wanted to convert into an ethnographic study. But he faced the problem of how to move from the amateur's interest to the professional's commitment. This issue is illustrated in Carlos Castaneda's description of his search for "the spot" (el sitio)—the place or area where the observer feels comfortable and is accepted and can begin to participate.[2] Boggs's quest for mentors in the world of salsa, or Afro-Hispanic music, was a version of that search.

Boggs died suddenly in 1994 while deeply engaged in field research on the origins of ethnic and racial crossover effects in popular music. We are proud to report that before his death he completed the study of salsa that he dreamed about in this epilogue. His book *Salsiology* contains many of the unique materials he collected during his productive and dedicated life as a sociologist "in the field."

NOTES

1. See James Clifford and George F. Marcus, eds., *Writing Culture: The Poetics and Politics of Ethnography* (Berkeley: University of California Press, 1986).

2. Carlos Castaneda, *The Teachings of Don Juan: A Yaqui Way of Knowledge* (New York: Simon & Schuster, 1973).

Part I

Gaining Entry

Jelly's Place

ELIJAH ANDERSON

"Jelly's" is a corner bar and liquor store in a poor black neighborhood on the South Side of Chicago. For three years Elijah Anderson observed the men at Jelly's, hanging out with both working and nonworking men who spent time in the bar. At all times of the day and night and throughout the year, Anderson socialized with the people at Jelly's, talking and listening to them and studying the patterns of interaction that occurred among them.

The purpose of Anderson's research was to discover the social order underlying the interactions among the men who frequented Jelly's. Among other things, he found that a man's rank at Jelly's was indicated by the degree of familiarity expressed in his speech and actions. This ranking process resulted in three fairly distinct categories: regulars (men who are steadily employed and have family ties), wineheads (men who are interested in "gettin' some wine" and "havin' some fun"), and hoodlums (men who care about being "tough" and getting "big money").

Since both Anderson and the men he was observing were black, it was somewhat easier for Anderson to gain acceptance than it might have been for a white observer. However, differences in social class constituted a barrier. When one man asked Anderson what he did for a living and was told that he was a student at the University of Chicago, his reaction was both proud and suspicious.

In this selection Anderson describes some of the interactions in which he participated, as well as the process through which he gained acceptance at Jelly's. In

This selection is adapted from Elijah Anderson, *A Place on the Corner.* Copyright © 1976, 1978 by The University of Chicago. Abridgment © 1989 by The University of Chicago. All rights reserved. Adapted with permission of The University of Chicago Press.

particular, it illustrates the importance of his relationship with Herman, one of the regulars. As often happens in field research, Herman sponsored Anderson; in the words of the men at Jelly's, the two "went for cousins."

Jelly's bar and liquor store has two front entrances, one leading to the barroom and the other to the liquor store. Each room has its own distinctive social character. The barroom is a public place; outfitted with bar stools, a marble-topped counter, and mirrors on the wall, it invites almost anyone to come and promises he will not be bothered as long as he minds his own business. In this sense it is a neutral social area. Yet people who gather on this side of Jelly's tend to be cautiously reserved when approaching others, mainly because on this side they just don't know one another. In contrast, the liquor store is more of a place for peers to hang out and outwardly appears to have a more easygoing, spontaneous ambience.

An open doorway separates the two rooms, and some people gravitate from side to side, the regular clientele usually settling in the liquor store. The social space of the barroom is shared by regular customers and visitors. Sometimes these visitors are people who have been seen around Jelly's but have yet to commit themselves to the setting. Sometimes they are total strangers. At times there will be as many as twenty visitors present, compared with eight or nine regular customers. Regular customers are interspersed among the visitors, but though the space is shared, they seldom come to know one another well. The visitors tend to arrive, get their drinks, sit at the bar for a while, then leave. The regular clientele, on the other hand, do their best to ignore the visitors; they treat them as interlopers. And there exists a certain amount of distrust and suspicion between the two groups.

The strange visitors of the barroom side are usually in the process of making their rounds to various drinking places on the South Side. They pass through Jelly's on their way to someplace else and have a relatively small social stake there. Most of them know few of the regular customers, and they usually do not know Jelly at all; those who do know him often know only that he is the owner of the place. Generally speaking, the regular customers see the visitors as outsiders in search of "action"—"on the hustle," as "trying to get over," or as "trying to get into something." Thus they tend to keep them at some distance and try to seek and maintain advantage during encounters. To the regular customers, the visitors, by and large, remain unknown. This makes for a certain amount of apprehension on the part of both groups and works to maintain distrust between them.

Although most of the visitors respect this definition of affairs, a visitor sometimes ventures into the liquor-store area and begins to hang. He is usually not encouraged to linger. When such a person enters, others usually stop talking or at least quiet down until he leaves. Their eyes follow him, reminding him that he is an intruder. Among the regular clientele he is regarded as an outsider, as one of "Jelly's customers," or even as "just a customer." Sensing that the liquor-store area is either beneath him or apart from him, or that it is too dangerous, the visitor usually finishes his business and returns to the barroom or goes on to another joint. Normally the visitors come to the bar, spend some time, then leave, remaining somewhat unknown to Jelly's regular clientele.

My first few weeks at Jelly's were spent on the barroom side among the visitors and others. This side, for the reasons just stated, was the place most accessible to new people, where strangers could congregate. It was also a place where I could be relatively unobtrusive, yet somewhat sociable. It was here that the process of getting to know Jelly's began, where increasingly I gained some license to exist and talk openly with people. Initially this meant getting to know the people and becoming somewhat involved in their relationships with one another; becoming familiar with the common, everyday understandings people shared and took for granted, the social rules and expectations they held for one another.

One of my earliest encounters was with a young man named Clarence, a visitor just passing through Jelly's. He asked me what I did for a living. I told him I was a student at the University of Chicago. He looked very surprised, but suspicious.

"When you get out of there, they got to treat you like a white man," he said. He was smiling gently, and he was sincere. He seemed both suspicious and a bit proud of my being at the university.

"How do you like it?" he asked cautiously.

"I like it all right," I said.

"You quite a ways from there, aren't you," he said in a half-stating, half-questioning way.

"Yeah, but I got a car," I said. "I come over here once in a while to get a drink and relax."

"Yeah, you got to get away from all them honkies after a while. I know how it is," he said. "Where do you stay?"

"Near Fifty-third and Harper," I answered.

"I know that area pretty good—used to hang out over there back in the fifties," he said. Clarence then mentioned some joints we both knew. From that point on we had easy conversation, laughing and talking, watching the people come and go.

Clarence offered to buy me a beer. I accepted and we kept talking. The jukebox blared and people continued to enter and leave, shouting, laughing, meeting friends. Rose, the barmaid, seemed to be enjoying her work, as she laughed and talked between serving up drinks.

As I finished each beer, Clarence would call to Rose and order another Schlitz for me and a gin and tonic for himself. I offered to buy some of the rounds, but he would not let me. For more than two hours we lounged around the barroom of Jelly's, watching the people come and go, gravitating from the barroom to the liquor store and back. The people seemed to be thoroughly enjoying themselves.

"You know, Eli, sometimes I regret I didn't finish high school and go to college. See, I didn't get no education. You got a good chance, you gettin' yourself educated and all, you gon' make something out o' yourself. Hell, get all you can, while you can. Don't be like me. Hell, I wish I could be in your place, goin' to school and all. But I tell you something else. You know, too much education is a bad thing. You can mess around and become a cranium. You ain't no cranium, are you? I hear some of them people at that university are really nutty—out there in left field somewhere. I hope you don't turn out like that. Get all you can, while you can, but don't turn into no cranium."

After a while our conversation drifted and dragged from topic to topic, and later I decided to go home. I thanked him for the drinks and told him that when I saw him again I would treat him. He told me not to worry about it; that he had really enjoyed talking. We parted and he went his way and I went mine.

The talk between Clarence and me, and the long and involved talks I had with so many other visitors, was more likely to have happened on the barroom side than in the liquor store. It is easier here in part because most of the visitors don't see one another again as buddies and thus may not have an immediate interest in status competition. In a social and emotional sense, their passing relationships can be very open to certain kinds of personal information.

During my first weeks on the barroom side, I became involved in many such conversations. Usually I never saw the person again or, if I did, the relationship would not pick up where it had left off. Seeming somewhat atomized on this side, most people did not seem to expect more than an agreeable and open ear from their counterparts. The visitors I had encountered on occasion came around once in a while, but when they did show up they were often somewhat detached and aloof from the center of things at Jelly's.

After I had been in the field at Jelly's for about four weeks I met Herman, a 45-year-old janitor. He wore a baggy army fatigue jacket, blue gabardine slacks, and black "keen-toed" shoes. On his head was a beige "high-boy" hat with a black band. Herman was a small brown-skinned man, about five feet eight inches tall and weighing about 145 pounds. At our first meeting I had been sitting at the bar for about twenty minutes, carrying on a conversation with Rose. Herman took the seat next to me and joined in the conversation. In this first encounter, Herman and I talked in much the same way as I had talked with other visitors to the barroom. At this point in the study, of course, I had not yet begun to make careful distinctions among the different types of people at Jelly's; the very notion of visitor, for instance, came to me only later. Herman was witty and seemed very easygoing, yet at times he spoke in a slow drawl. He impressed me as a person experienced on the ghetto streets, for his conversation was spiced with well-placed references to such experiences. Because of my previous encounters in the barroom, which on the whole had not been outstandingly productive, I at first took Herman as just another person I probably would not see again. But, as I was to find out, Herman was not just another visitor, but a member of the regular clientele of Jelly's.

In the course of our initial encounter Herman and I talked briefly but became very involved. Among other things, he mentioned that he had seen me around before, though I had not noticed him. During this conversation, his questions centered on the issue of what I was doing there. Although he never stated this directly, he did ask some leading questions. Not broaching it at first, he led up to it in a subtle conversation of gestures and words. Interested in "who I was," Herman asked me, "What do you do, Eli?" He wanted to know how I spent my time and whether I was gainfully employed. As I was to discover, around Jelly's whether someone works for a living is an important clue to his definition. For most people this helps to determine whether he is to be trusted within the setting, and to what degree.

In response to Herman's inquiries about my occupation, I said, "I'm a graduate student over at the University of Chicago."

"That's nice," said Herman, seeming a little surprised. "How long you been over there?" As I answered his question, he seemed to take this as a kind of license to ask more and more about me. And I took his inquiries as cues that I could do the same. Taking this license, I asked him more about himself. During this exchange of information I noticed a marked change in Herman's demeanor toward me. He became more relaxed and sure of me. He gestured more as he spoke, punctuating his words with hits and jabs to my shoulder. He was a very friendly and affable man. At times I reciprocated by punctuating my own words with smiles and friendly exclamations. On the ghetto streets and in ghetto bars friendly students are not to be feared and suspected but are generally expected to be "square" and bookish. With all the information he had about me, including my willingness to give it, he could place me as "safe" within his own scheme of standards and values.

My openness encouraged Herman to be open with me. As a result, there was now some basis for trust in our relationship. In telling me more about himself, Herman said he was a janitor but quickly added, "I'm a man among men," implying that, contrary to what some might expect of a janitor, he held himself in high esteem. Then he told me about his work and about how early he had to get up in the morning. After more of this familiarizing talk, we parted company on good terms. We had spent more than two hours laughing and talking together. I had held this kind of information exchange with others before, and I didn't expect anything unusual to come from this particular meeting. But it was encounters like this that made me conscious that who I was and how I fit into the cognitive picture of Jelly's did preoccupy some of its more persistent members. When I went to Jelly's the next day, I met Herman again. As I entered the barroom I greeted Rose and others as I usually did. I took a seat at the bar and from my stool watched the activities of the men in the liquor-store room.

In that room people were engaged in spontaneous fun—laughing, yelling, playing with one another, and being generally at ease. To me that room seemed very exciting, but it was clear that I would have been out of place there for it seemed to be only for peer-group members. I sensed that there I would have been reminded of my outsider status again and again. While in the barroom, among the visitors and a few of the peer-group members who gravitated over now and then, I felt *in place*. Looking into the liquor-store room, I saw Herman. Catching his attention, I beckoned to him, and he came over to me in the barroom. We shook hands and greeted each other, then held a friendly conversation over a couple of beers. But soon he returned to the liquor-store area, where more of his buddies seemed to be. That Herman had buddies, and so many of them, was one of the important distinctions between him and many of the visitors I had previously met at Jelly's.

In contrast to the visitors on the barroom side of Jelly's, the regular customers on the liquor-store side tend to be spontaneous, loud, and relatively sure of themselves during interactions. Herman and the others acted very much at home there—and they were. Herman was a very sociable person and seemed to be in and out of everyone's affairs. I could see that very little went on at Jelly's without his knowledge. Recognizing this turned out to have important consequences for my entree to the social world of Jelly's, for it was clear that not many new people stayed around without his soon getting to know them. It became apparent that Jelly's was very much Herman's place; it was his turf, a place where he felt protected from the wrong kind of outsiders.

Apparently he saw me as the right kind of outsider, because when I saw him again in a few days, Herman invited me to share his turf. Again, I was sitting in the barroom, while Herman was laughing and talking with a group of men in the liquor-store room. When I saw them through the open doorway that divided the two areas, I was about to leave. I decided to go through the liquor store to greet Herman, but also to get a closer view of the activity of that room.

As I approached the men I heard Herman say, "Hey, here come my friend, Eli!" Then he said to Sleepy, one of the other men, "He al'right. Hey, this the stud I been tellin' you about. This cat gettin' his doctor's degree." At this point Herman shook my hand and greeted me. I returned the greeting. The others of the group seemed cautious and somewhat incredulous about accepting the "me" presented by Herman. Yet they were polite and approving and remained silent while he and I went through the greeting action. The men just watched, checking us out and talking among themselves. Shortly, Herman began introducing me to the others.

"Hey, Eli. Meet Jake, T. J., and this here's Sleepy." The men then acknowledged me, nodding and saying their hellos. I exchanged greetings with them.

Herman, beer in hand, boasted to the men about a Christmas party he was going to attend where he worked. To make it especially meaningful he accentuated the occasion, describing it as something extravagant and special. He talked of the "foxy chicks" he would be kissing under the mistletoe and of the "intelligent folks" he would be "conversin' " with. Jake responded by saying, "Aw, that nigger's crazy." Other responses were similar, but Herman persisted.

At one point in his presentation Herman invited me to the Christmas party.

"Hey, Eli. You wanna come to a Christmas party tomorrow?"

"What's this?" I answered, surprised at the invitation.

"The place I work gon' have a Christmas party tomorrow. Gon' be some real fine foxes there, some good whiskey, too," said Herman.

"Sure, I'll come. What time?"

"Meet me at 2:30 at _____, OK?"

"I'll be there," I said.

The men of the group continued to check us out. Herman was treating me as a friend, as an insider, as though my status in the group were somehow already assured. Certainly Herman would not invite just anyone to a party at work. Other group members wouldn't have expected this and in fact would have been surprised if he had asked one of them. After this demonstration by Herman, I could feel the others in the group warm up to me; they looked at me more directly and seemed to laugh more easily.

I began to feel comfortable enough to stand around in the group and listen to the banter, but not to participate in it, my reticence reflecting my sense of my visitor status. But I did laugh and talk with the fellows, trying to get to know people I had often wondered about during the past four or five weeks. These were people I had seen around but had never before attempted to "be with." After a while I told Herman and my new friends I had to be getting home.

For me the evening had been remarkable. It was the first time I had been introduced to anyone well connected within the social setting of Jelly's; the first time I had actually been sponsored by someone with an important social stake there. And no less significant, it was my first social venture on the liquor-store side of Jelly's—a real achievement. I had become involved with peer-group members, people for whom others at Jelly's really mattered. The whole experience marked the real beginning of my entree: It was the time from which I began to gain a feeling of place at Jelly's.

When Herman sponsored me and invited me to the party, I assumed some usefulness for and responsibility toward him. As I was to learn, one thing I could give Herman was verification of his role at the party—and of the identity that went along with it.

When I arrived at his place of work on the day of the party, Herman showed me around the buildings he kept clean as janitor. He led me from room to room, from hallway to hallway, and from floor to floor, taking great pride in their immaculate look. As he showed me around, he said in an aside that he would have to introduce me to others as his "cousin," since he could not let "just anybody" in there. I agreed to be his "cousin," which was still a dubious status in the minds of those we were to encounter at the party, if not in Herman's mind. But this was Herman's show. He was the director.

Before introducing me around Herman quietly asked me my mother's name. I told him. Then he told me his mother's name, and assured me all the while that this was "just in case somebody don't believe us." In exchanging our mothers' names, though, Herman and I demonstrated a certain degree of trust. Such confidential information is not generally disclosed to just anyone without reservation.

Another important point suggested by Herman's careful preparation of our story is that those at Jelly's who attempt a venturesome self-presentation have learned that they must expect to be seriously challenged. Hence they feel pressured to "have their shit together"—that is, to have a convincing and ready account of who they are. In the peer group at Jelly's this means that a person who expects to have his version of his identity taken seriously must have a "strong rap" (an impressive verbal account of himself) prepared, with good illustrations, details, and evidence.

In the world outside Jelly's—for example, at his place of work—Herman employs his own notions of what it takes to be believed, to be taken seriously, and to protect himself from being "shot down" or "blown away." These notions, grounded in Herman's experience on the streets around Jelly's, are the background to his careful preparation of our "story" for the people at the Christmas party.

At the party, Herman introduced me as his cousin who "goes to the University of Chicago, gettin' his Ph.D." He even told one black secretary that I was the cousin he had long been telling her about. Herman was the only janitor at the party; the others present were professionals and office workers. He and I were the only representatives from any setting at all like Jelly's. Yet with Herman's direction we moved easily among these people. With each introduction he beamed with pride over his "cousin, who's gettin' his Ph.D."

When the affair was over and we were leaving, Herman said to me, "I'm a man among men," declaring his own sense of accomplishment and self-esteem. Obviously, he felt that the whole show had been a great success. As we walked to my car, he repeated, "Yeah, I feel like a man among men. Eli, I knew you was a decent stud when I first met you. Now, you don't owe me nothing, you didn't have to come, but you came. You my best friend, hear?" Herman was elated at the success of his show and at how he had impressed the people "at work." As we were driving back to Jelly's Herman told me why he had chosen me to come to the party, rather than any of his buddies at Jelly's. "I wouldn't trust none o' them studs comin' all up on my job. Them cats don't know how to act 'round decent folks and intelligent folks. And sometimes I ain't so sure 'bout myself, 'specially if I get a little high on. Might get up there and start actin' a damn fool. Ha-ha." But Herman was sure about me. He was convinced that I knew how to act around "decent folks and intelligent folks." After all, I had "all that education." But equally important, I could come back and report to all the fellows at Jelly's, especially "ol' fat-assed Jelly" himself, about how we had partied with "decent folks at the Christmas party." He reminded me to do just that as he got out of my car.

When I did return to Jelly's, I told the fellows of the peer group how Herman and I had partied. With this verification of his story and, in a sense, of the identity he wanted them to know, I became all the more closely linked with him around Jelly's. All of this made a big hit there, and Herman's rank, at least when the outside world was the issue, became a little less precarious.

Group members seemed to accept my verification of Herman's adventures at work. Now when he spoke about "partying," people listened and were not as disparaging as they had been the day he invited me to the party. For the time being, at least to his face, the men seemed to have called a moratorium on attempting to "shoot him down" on this issue.

Thereafter Herman referred to me as his cousin and introduced me to others that way. In a sense this was the place I had lobbied for, however unwittingly. We hung together and treated each other as close friends, and the men followed suit. The more I hung with Herman and verified his stories, the closer we seemed to become. We began to "go for cousins," as the men say. Many of the men knew, of course, that we were not real cousins, and, perhaps even more important, Herman knew they knew. This was not a case of deception. Rather, the fictive kinship term of cousin was used by Herman, as it is by so many men on the streets around Jelly's, to signify that we were close friends.

One of the important implicit aspects of this developing relationship concerned its protective nature. Herman and I would often hang together and leave Jelly's together to go home or to a movie or somewhere else. Among peer-group members, an unspoken rule requires those who hang together to help or "take up for" one another in times of need—particularly during physical fights, but also on general social matters. My relationship with Herman gave me a certain implicit status in the group, a place interconnected with the "rep" and rank Herman was sensed to have. A set of mutual obligations and expectations began to form, so that group members expected us to take up for each other.

My growing awareness of these developments contributed to my own self-confidence around Jelly's liquor-store room, as I slowly secured a right to be there. During the course of this entree, I increasingly came under Herman's tutelage and guardianship. But why did Herman engage me in friendship at all? What was in it for him? After getting to know Herman better, I became aware that he regards himself as very knowledgeable about the ghetto streets. There is a certain amount of esteem to be gained by demonstrating that one knows his way around the streets, and Herman sees and presents himself as someone who has been "through it all."

Born and raised in Chicago, Herman has spent a good part of his life coming to terms with "the streets." He has been "through World War II," has been "a pimp, a hustler, a junkie" among other things—and has survived to talk about it all, something he does whenever "the streets" becomes an issue around Jelly's.

Because he carries this extensive and widely known personal biography, Herman is able to command a certain measure of esteem from the men who constitute Jelly's regular clientele. Other regulars usually agree with this definition of him and will work collectively to maintain it. At the same time, Herman wants to see himself as "decent." However, he knows that such an identity is difficult to maintain for anyone hanging out at Jelly's.

In our relationship I provided Herman with a kind of verification of his identity and status on the streets and in "decent" society. Specifically, as I provided him with a "decent" pupil, one who had "all that education," I reflected well upon him and could thus verify his own claims to "decency." Of course I could also verify Herman's claims to street prowess by allowing him to teach me about the streets. And this really was important to me, since I needed to know the streets if I were to survive and carry out my fieldwork. By taking me under his wing, Herman could show that he knew the streets very well and at the same time could "be somebody" when "decent" friends became the issue.

All this fit nicely with the low-key, nonassertive role I assumed at the beginning of my study. I behaved in this way to prevent unwieldy challenges from those who might have felt threatened by a more aggressive demeanor, especially from a stranger. It is the kind of role any outsider must play—is forced into—if he is not to disrupt the consensual definition of social order in this type of setting.

Doing Research in The Flats

CAROL STACK

Carol Stack was one of the first social scientists to explore the functions of the kinship network in low-income communities. During the mid-1960s she conducted an extensive study of The Flats, the poorest section of a black community in the midwestern city of Jackson Harbor (both names are fictitious). Many of the residents had migrated to Jackson Harbor from the South in the 1930s and 1940s. Their hopes for a better life had been disappointed, and they had spent a lifetime in poverty. The same was true for their children and grandchildren.

Many of the residents of The Flats were unemployed, and most of those who were employed had low-paying service jobs and were not much better off than those who were eligible for welfare benefits. They lived in small, crowded, run-down wood-frame houses and shacks; the streets and yards were littered with broken glass, beer cans, and old cars.

Stack spent three years in close company with several women who lived in The Flats. She visited with them in their homes and accompanied them to clinics and welfare offices, day care centers, churches, and local markets. Gradually she became part of a "personal network" of friends in whose households she was welcome. In the course of her research she became intensely aware of the importance of such networks in the lives of the residents.

An important finding of Stack's research was that families in The Flats regarded many non-kin individuals as kin and included them in kinship-based exchange networks that linked together numerous domestic units. The community was also characterized by elastic household boundaries and lifelong bonds to three-generation households. These and other features of life in The Flats helped the residents adapt to a life of poverty, unemployment, and welfare dependency. In fact, Stack's report on her research, All Our Kin, *is subtitled* Strategies for Survival in a Black Community.

Like other researchers whose accounts are included in this volume, Stack faced the question of whether a white observer could ever be fully accepted in a black community. Eventually, as this selection shows, she was accepted—under the name of "white Caroline."

In both industrial and nonindustrial societies, researchers have typically established their first contacts with men who hold power—the colonial administrators, tribal chiefs, local mayors, and judges. These men draw upon their status in the community and favors owed to them to usher the researchers into the community, the first link in what becomes a chain of introductions. Anyone proceeding through other channels runs the risk of offending those in power and provoking an invitation to leave the community.

Within most black communities in the United States today, power is divided among the older generation of professionals in the black estab-lishment and the younger activist leaders and organizations. I could have gained my first contacts in The Flats by working through the established network of black men and women who had status and power in The Flats and in the larger community of Jackson Harbor. In the mid-sixties two other white social scientists had entered the black community in Jackson Harbor through contacts with preachers, teachers, social workers, and other black professionals. Although they were not conducting a study re-quiring intensive participant-observer techniques, their research was con-fined and limited. They came into contact only with individuals and fami-lies chosen by the black establishment to represent the community: churchgoers, families on good terms with their social workers, and those men and women who had obtained legal marriages. Even more decisive as a handicap was their identification, in the eyes of those studied, with those black leaders who personally derived their status and importance from their acceptance within the white community. They were regarded as "uppity" individuals who "thought they were too good to sit down on an old couch."

When I first began this study in the mid-sixties, the community itself had produced a few articulate, intellectual spokesmen against racial and political injustice. Their speeches and their activities were aimed primar-ily at the white community. Within the black community itself, they were not controlling voices. I later came to know the young men and women involved in political activism within the black community as I became committed to their causes: a free health center, a Welfare Rights Organization, a job-training center, black businesses. Many of these individuals whom I met in the initial stages of this research later became members of activist organizations in The Flats. Such persons may, in the future, decide whether a research study of their community may be conducted and by whom. They may choose to censor findings that they believe may be used to repress, harm, or manipulate those studied.

Some of my colleagues strongly advised me to enter the black community through the older black establishment; they cited various reasons: Contacts were available; the research setting, they argued, was physically dangerous to a white person and I might need the sponsorship and protection that such contacts could provide; and tradition dictated such a procedure. I decided instead to find my own means of entree. I decided to circumvent the obvious centers of influence—the pastors, the politicians—and try to reach families without resorting to middlemen. Through my own efforts and good luck I came to know a young woman who had grown up on welfare in The Flats and had since come to my university. She agreed to introduce me to families she had known as she was growing up there. She would introduce me to two unrelated families and from then on I would be on my own.

In time I knew enough people well who were closely related so that after any family scene, gathering, or fight, I could put together interpretations of the events from the viewpoints of different individuals, particularly in instances when there were conflicts over rights in children. In addition to taking multiple observations of each event myself, I eventually asked others to assist me in the study. I found three Flats residents (two women and a man) who participated as part-time and casual assistants in the project. I selected individuals from the families I knew, who were interested in the study, and who were imaginative and critical thinkers. Together we worked out questions on various topics to ask the families studied.

We selected questions in the general areas of social and domestic relations, kinship and residence, and child-keeping; these questions provided a starting point for long discussions on a single issue. At no time did I formally interview anyone. I taped informal conversations after an event, when I was alone with someone I knew and with permission, asking that the situation be related to me from that person's point of view.

Because of the personal nature of the information obtained about individuals, and the promise that this information would be confidential, it was necessary to disguise the names of the informants. I gave a fictitious name to each person whose name or life entered into the study. Even when I tried out my own assumptions and interpretations of events on my friends and assistants, I used fictitious names for the examples.

The people that I studied in The Flats use first names in one another's presence, and to refer to their neighbors and friends. Surnames are used infrequently and often people do not know the surnames of long-time acquaintances and friends, although the coining of nicknames for siblings and friends is a creative and endless pastime. Nicknames personalize and endear; they dramatically expose memorable or striking characteristics about a person, giving him a very special identity. I also acquired several nicknames during the study, but the one that held was "white Caroline," a name originally given to me by a family to distinguish me from their niece whose name was also Caroline. (My real name, Carol, was always pronounced *Caroline*.) She became known as "black Caroline" soon after the children in her family began calling me "white Caroline." I first discovered this nickname one afternoon when I phoned the family and the youngster who answered the phone called out, "Mama, white Caroline's on the phone."

Members of a culture have biases that affect their perceptions of themselves and their life ways; outsiders bring biases to the cultures they study. Although life experiences produce a difference in perceptions, these perceptions can be shared. The three years I spent in The Flats opened and reassembled my life ways and my understanding of womanhood, parenthood, and the American economy. Likewise, I brought perceptions and biases to the study that joggled and molded the views of those closest to me.

A researcher in the social sciences is practically always defined as an outsider in a study, even if he or she has close attachment and commitment to the community, and shares a similar cultural background. Even a study of the culture of one's most intimate associations—our friends, colleagues, or kin—thrusts the researcher apart. Whether studying elites, bureaucracy, or the poor, if one hopes to discover the rules of routine behavior, the observer himself must attempt to learn how to move appropriately inside the private world of those observed. The researcher must take time and patience and practice, attempting to reduce the distance between the model outsiders use to explain social order and the explanations employed by those studied. Attempts will fail, but this prodding hopefully will bring the observer to an intimate point of contact in the study whereby he becomes both an actor and a subject whose learned definitions can themselves be analyzed.

An important stage of my research began when my car broke down. Despite the fact that the car was a convenience—it gave me an easily explainable role in the lives of the families I knew, helping me provide daily assistance with the children, the shopping, the problems with "papers," the welfare office, sick children, and so on—when it broke down I decided not to fix it. Without the car, my presence in the community was less apparent. I was able to spend long days in the homes of people I had met, participating in their daily lives. I had already developed tentative hypotheses on the style of social relations in The Flats and on the ways in which people expand their network of exchange. I began to focus my attention on how networks were expanded, who the participants were, and how residents in The Flats see and interpret this process.

My role in the community at this point was no longer that of an outsider. To many families I became another link in the systems of exchanges that were part of their existence. Viola Jackson's sisters once told me that people look at you when you have a white friend, saying that you are really on the white man's side and that you do everything they want you to do. But Ophelia said to me that people understand what friendship means. Friends can ask any favor of one another, any time of the night, and it shouldn't make any difference. No one would tell you to drop a friend you can trust even if she is white. Ruby Banks told me that from the first day we started going around together, people said that we looked alike and that we did so much together that we seemed just "like sisters." Our affinity influenced the behavior of Ruby's kin toward me and their persistent concern for my well-being. It also influenced Ruby's behavior toward me in public settings within and outside the ghetto. When Ruby's youngest child was sick in the local hospital, we went to visit her. The first day, the white nurse on duty stopped me—the rules stated that only close relatives could visit. Ruby told the nurse angrily, "Caroline here is my sister, and nothing's stopping her from visiting this baby." Ruby's claim went unchallenged, and we were able to visit the baby every day.

Exploring the Cocaine Culture

TERRY WILLIAMS

Terry Williams is an African-American sociologist who is widely regarded as a master of street-level ethnography. He has investigated the hopes and dreams of unemployed teenagers, the interactions of proprietors and patrons in pornography establishments, and the subculture of cocaine users in after-hours clubs. It is the latter research that forms the subject of this selection.

A guiding principle of Williams's research is the desire to take the insider's point of view rather than approaching his subject with the preconceived ideas of an outsider. In order to see the world through the eyes of the insider, he must become intimate with the people he is observing. In fact, he becomes part of their life; they are no longer "subjects" or informants but friends and associates.

Williams was relatively inexperienced when he undertook his study of the cocaine culture, and he learned many lessons the hard way. Especially troublesome were the ethical implications of the research—whether he had a right to observe individuals engaging in a private (and illegal) activity, and whether his role as a reporter of those activities would later create problems for those who trusted him with privileged information. There was also the matter of risk: There can be no doubt that Williams was in considerable danger on several occasions while conducting his study.

One outcome of Williams's research in the after-hours clubs was that it led to further research on cocaine use. In the 1970s he became aware of a new way of using the drug, known as free-basing, which turned out to be a precursor of the "crack" epidemic of recent years. Thus, although The Blue Cat Cafe *was never published, Williams went on to write* The Cocaine Kids, *which was published by Addison-Wesley in 1989. The latter work includes what Williams calls "dramatic portraits" of young cocaine dealers that portray the "kids" as they see themselves.*

The following account contains several illustrations of the process through which Williams learned how to locate and interact with members of the cocaine users' subculture.

In 1974, after completing several years of graduate study in sociology at the City University of New York, I accepted a teaching position at John Jay College of Criminal Justice. My first assignment entailed commuting from the main campus to Rikers Island to teach in the satellite program established by the college. After a year in this special program, I became friendly with several of the inmates, many of whom were serving relatively light sentences. Upon their release, three of them called me and offered to take me out on the town.

They showed me the nightlife of New York City as I had never seen it before. In small, intimate clubs known as after-hours spots, I was introduced to a bewildering variety of people—musicians, drug dealers, punk rockers, transvestites, secretaries, doctors, dancers, gamblers, actors, policemen, prostitutes—all of whom were there to share in a lifestyle based on the enjoyment of cocaine and the pleasure and excitement brought on by the intensity of their interaction. I mentioned this experience to some of my colleagues and mentors at the CUNY Graduate Center, and they encouraged me to conduct a systematic study of cocaine use in after-hours clubs.

On a few occasions early in my research I traveled alone through forbidding city streets in the hope of gaining entry to a club on my own. But the clubs are private enterprises with a distinctive clientele. Among other things, dress is an important criterion in establishing membership; time after time I was denied entry because I lacked the proper attire. I needed to wear leather, suede, or other elegant clothing, and avoid the collegiate look. Since I could not afford these accoutrements, I adopted the strategy of giving a name or nickname that is fairly commonly used by patrons of after-hours clubs, such as Iceman, Cool Breeze, Mr. T, Jack, Slick, or Country. There are always people with names like these in the community of hustlers. Sometimes I gave the name of a person I knew to be a member of a particular club, and occasionally this strategy worked, but many times it did not.

On those occasions when I succeeded in gaining entry to a club, I made an effort to become acquainted with the doorman, barmaids, and patrons. After eight months in the field, I became friendly with the doorman at a club in midtown Manhattan. It turned out that he knew dozens of people in clubs throughout the city. His name became my password; it guaranteed entry into his club (when he was not working there) and several others.

Getting into the clubs did not automatically give me access to a new set of contacts; quite the contrary. I had to be especially careful not to appear overly friendly or curious, yet I knew that direct experiential involvement with key members of the clubs was essential. I knew that building rapport was the single most important dynamic in an otherwise difficult social world. I knew, too, that I must interact with at least one person who attended the club on a regular basis. I had to become something more than an observer; otherwise I would be under the continual scrutiny of owner/managers and many of the patrons.

To accomplish this goal I had to identify something within the cocaine culture that would allow me to interact with club members without using cocaine. I observed several patrons actually refusing cocaine that was offered them, saying "my nose is out" or "I'm coked out" or simply that they did not trust other people's drugs. Using this technique, which fit the norms of the subculture I was observing, allowed me to interact without attracting suspicion and at the same time to gain a measure of unanticipated respect from dealers who felt that many patrons took advantage of the ceremonial offering of cocaine and became "overindulgers" or "vacuum cleaner sniffers."

In this way I became a participant observer of cocaine users in after-hours clubs. As a patron of the clubs, I could observe how people use cocaine in their face-to-face relations with others. There being no standard rules for a study of this nature, I had to establish several for myself. They were as follows:

1. Avoid using all drugs.
2. Establish solid rapport with key persons.
3. Avoid pretension, be yourself.
4. Ask people what names they give themselves (e.g., cokehead, player, businessman, dealer).
5. Do not label indiscriminately or stereotype.
6. Do not betray the trust of your contacts.

Even with these rules, my research was plagued with problems of ethics as well as some very real dangers. I had no illusions about the dangers of research on drug users and was then, as I am now, concerned about the possible legal and legislative consequences of this kind of research. I drew some (but not much) consolation from the realization that people have been using cocaine and gathering in after-hours clubs for over a century and will probably continue to do so even in the face of legal and other obstacles.

Some of the ramifications of research of this kind became evident on two occasions, one past and one recent. The recent occasion involved a trial in which I was an expert witness and was asked to name one of my informants, a major heroin and cocaine dealer. I refused and was held in contempt of court by a federal judge. I was not remanded to jail because I produced a letter of confidentiality that essentially made my notes and contacts immune from prosecution by virtue of their anonymity.

In the earlier instance, I was in a Brooklyn club where I was already conspicuous as a nonuser of cocaine. It seems that I was also overzealous, in the sense that I was staring too much and asking too many questions. One of the club's owners came over to me and said, "Listen, my man, if you're undercover, I got people that'll take care of that." I was not sure whether he meant force or bribery, but in any case I stopped going to that club.

On another occasion I was in a club that had been heterosexual until the Thursday night I arrived, which was "gay night." I thought I would take advantage of the situation for sociological purposes, making comparisons between heterosexual and homosexual cocaine users. I was wearing black leather (the fashion in New York at the time), not realizing the role of black leather in the gay community. I noticed a group of men sitting in a corner and moved toward them inconspicuously, or so I thought, until I was eight or ten feet away. One of them stared up at me and I of course looked toward him. His sleeves were rolled past his elbows, revealing purple and red tattoos on both arms. After looking at me for a few seconds, he walked over and offered to buy me a drink, asking if this was my first time there. I explained that I had been there before and informed him that I was a researcher and just wanted to talk to as many people as possible. He grew red in the face and said to his companions in a loud voice, hands on hips, head cocked to one side, "Hey, get a load of this one. He wants to do research on us. You scum bag! What do we look like, pal? Fucking guinea pigs? You got some nerve walking in here, talking about doing some research!"

By this time everyone in the place was staring at me and I was embarrassed and a bit shaken up by the turn of events. I went over to the bar and the bartender said to me, "Don't mind Wayne, he's off duty [a policeman] and likes to throw his weight around."

It was at times like these that I seriously questioned facets of my methodological approach. This was only one of many such incidents (which fortunately never became violent) that occurred during my initial fieldwork. It did not take me long to realize that this approach would not work. I then decided to be selective in informing people of my purpose; I would inform others about my findings after the research was completed. This plan has been all but impossible to carry out. Many of the clubs I visited have either closed or moved to new locations unknown to me. Many of the patrons have moved on; some have died; others have gone to prison. The after-hours club has a transient quality that I was not aware of at the beginning of my study.

My observations of cocaine users in clubs suggested that the dealers who supply them with the drug are as significant as the club itself. Although the clubs' managers often sold cocaine to patrons, most users obtained their cocaine from dealers outside the clubs so that they could give it away inside in the ritual sharing snorters engage in. Therefore, to supplement my understanding of the cocaine culture in the after-hours clubs, I conducted interviews with a number of dealers. Many dealers were unwilling to act as contacts because they feared that I would be unable to guarantee confidentiality. Nevertheless, there were some who had a story to tell, and I was there to listen.

As a researcher, I knew what data I needed: information on cocaine users and the associated nightlife, street myths about use and pharmacology, emerging trends, and other elements of cultural lore. But as most researchers know, there is a quid pro quo in every research situation. What the researcher wants is not always what the contact desires in exchange. I was asked to do a variety of favors, such as lending money and finding lawyers, social workers, doctors, painters, apartments, caterers, and clothing stores. On many occasions I was asked to engage in illegal acts. The most memorable of those occurred when I was at the home of a dealer whom I will call Alfredo. The phone rang and Alfredo had a heated argument with the caller. After hanging up, he waited a few choice seconds, then looked me in the eye and said, "Listen, a guy is coming over here and I owe him money. He wants what I owe him in coke. I told him I didn't have any blow [cocaine], but somebody told him I did. Now I told him my friend is here and he has some, but it's expensive. All I want you to do is hold this bag [it contained about 2 ounces of cocaine], and when he comes tell him it's yours and it'll cost him $1,500—no more, no less. Don't bat an eyelash no matter what he does or says."

Before I could say anything, the doorbell rang and a friend of Alfredo's whom I had met previously arrived. They both started to laugh, saying that the whole episode had been a joke for the purpose of testing me.

This and similar requests put me in an awkward position, and I have often thought about this as if it were not a joke. What if there really had been someone to whom Alfredo owed money—a situation that occurred frequently in his life as a dealer—and that person knew the kinds of games Alfredo played? There are many "what if's" in this type of research. Yet even though I felt that it was inappropriate—not to mention illegal and dangerous—to perform such services, I could not refuse what appeared to Alfredo to be a simple favor—especially after he had given me access to information that could send him to jail for life.

This kind of research, in which one both observes and becomes part of the group under study, is called ethnography, participant observation, qualitative research, or field study by social scientists, and advanced journalism by their critics. Ethnography is the science of cultural description;

more than that, it is a methodology. It is a way of looking at people, a way of looking at a culture. It is recording how people perceive, construct, and interact in their own private world. It embraces the subjective reality of the individuals it seeks to understand. It defines the group the way the group defines itself.

But cocaine use, because it is illegal, cannot be examined in isolation from the society in which it occurs. Every sniff of cocaine is an act of rebellion, an act performed in defiance of the law. The hidden dissent of cocaine users, and of drug dealers more generally, is just one aspect of the symbolic dissent in which many Americans are participating in the late twentieth century. The corporate executive, the coffee shop owner, the fashion designer, the corrupt police officer, the restaurant owner— all evade taxes, use illegal drugs, and beat the system in one way or another. The interactions of individuals in cocaine clubs, thus, are part of a larger mosaic that includes such forces as class conflict and social control.

Within this context, I explored the night-time world of cocaine users with scholarly interest. In the hundreds of hours I spent in after-hours clubs I was able to discover, penetrate, and examine this world with few distractions. I became acquainted with the after-hours life of fear, risk, desire, disapproval, and revolt. I sought to grasp it, to touch even its more dangerous side. At the same time, I was standing outside of this secret world, counting and categorizing, measuring and comparing. I was trying to understand the cocaine culture without becoming absorbed by it.

In the Field with Snake Handlers

PEGGY SULLIVAN and KIRK ELIFSON

Ethnographers Peggy Sullivan and Kirk Elifson began the study from which this selection is taken almost by accident. What began as a visit to a church out of simple curiosity grew into a two-year research project. As they describe it, they attended a service of the Free Holiness, a small group of Pentecostal Christians for whom serpent handling is a key element of religious observance. Fascinated by what they saw, they obtained permission to conduct further observation and interviews in a study that eventually became the subject of Sullivan's master's thesis.

The Free Holiness place strong emphasis on a literal interpretation of Mark 16: 17–18: "And these signs shall follow them that believe; In my name shall they cast out devils; they shall speak with new tongues; they shall take up serpents; and if they drink any deadly thing, it shall not hurt them; they shall lay hands on the sick and they shall recover." Their belief in the literal truth of these statements is clearly evident in the practices described in this selection.

Sullivan and Elifson were interested in the Free Holiness as a deviant subculture. They wanted to know how the group's members identified themselves, how they maintained the boundaries between themselves and others, and how they emphasized their uniqueness through their songs and sermons and in their daily lives. After two years of research they felt close to their subjects and had come to respect them even though they could not accept their belief system.

The authors note that an important and often overlooked aspect of ethnographic research is thorough planning. A study of this type must be approached carefully. It is necessary to win over the leadership first, especially when studying a group with strong leaders. In addition, candor is essential in seeking entry into a world quite different from one's own. In this instance, the ethnographers' openness was reflected in the trust relationship they were able to establish with church members.

A thorough examination of the methods used in any research project shows them not to be nearly as neat and orderly as methodology texts prescribe. A study of a serpent handling church in rural Georgia was no exception. What began as a curiosity visit grew into a two-year research project. Kirk originally went to the church with an undergraduate class he was teaching and later returned with graduate students from a sociology of religion seminar. Peggy was among those students. We arrived and sat on the last pew near the back door. Our curiosity was mixed with trepidation as we waited for the service to begin.

The entire service seemed very foreign. We were often unable to understand what was happening at the front of the church. The songs were unfamiliar to us and we had difficulty understanding the words; however, we did stand and clap in time with the music. Prayers were so loud and individualistic that a cacophony prevailed. Those around us often appeared to be in a frenzied state and far removed from the world we knew. Later we decided that the entire service had been such a cultural shock for us that by the time they handled the snakes we were in a mildly dissociative state ourselves and the snake handling did not seem as frightening as it might have been otherwise.

The believers only handle poisonous snakes and prefer rattlesnakes, copperheads, cottonmouths, and water moccasins. During the service while several men were handling snakes, a small copperhead bit a young man on the hand. He shook his hand vigorously as if to relieve the pain and used a handkerchief to wipe the blood that dripped from the wound. The service continued at an even higher pitch after he was bitten. Singing, praying, and laying on of hands occurred as the attention of the church shifted to focus on the victim. Later he left the altar area, washed the blood from his hand, and returned to his seat as the service continued.

FEASIBILITY OF THE RESEARCH

At first it was a half-joke-half-dare between us that we should conduct a participant observation research project focused on the church. Several days after the seminar group had visited the church we decided to learn if studying the church would be possible. We knew practically nothing about rural Pentecostal religion and even less about serpent handlers. We had no idea whether we would be welcomed to the church enough to study it. A literature search yielded little information. Because there was a possibility of seriously studying the church, we decided to begin taking notes about our initial experiences and impressions while they were still clear.

We carefully planned our next contact with the church. We felt we should first approach the church leaders with our intentions and wrote a brief letter to the church's minister asking to meet with him to talk about his church. We followed the letter with a call and the minister not only agreed to talk with us but invited us to his home before the Saturday evening service. In his small living room we sat and talked with the minister and another elderly snake handling minister who was visiting from Virginia's coal mining area. Both men loved to talk about serpent handling and we were kept spellbound by their stories. The local preacher's wife sat in on the conversation but spoke very little. The preacher insisted that we eat dinner with his family and they treated us to a country dinner of fried chicken, mashed potatoes, biscuits, and apple cobbler. The blessing before the meal amazed us as simultaneously each person said an individual prayer aloud and the preachers both began to speak in tongues.

In spite of the reason for our afternoon meeting with the minister, neither of us broached the topic of studying the church. On our return to Atlanta that evening we were ashamed to admit that we had avoided the topic. We soon realized that our cowardly hesitation probably served us well because we had begun to establish a rapport that led to a tacit understanding that we were welcome. Had we been more direct before they knew us better, they would likely have refused us.

METHODOLOGICAL DECISIONS

Our first visits were in May and we originally hoped to be out of the field by the end of the summer. This timetable, in retrospect, was naive and unrealistic. It was based on the experience of survey researchers, not participant observers. We began going to church at least once and often twice a week and soon realized how unreasonable our initial timetable was. We discovered the importance of moving very slowly at first in order to build rapport and spent the first few months primarily listening.

After our initial visit with the preacher we decided to be very open about our research and explained exactly what we intended to do. We elected not to try to disguise ourselves as converts or even potential converts. We told the church members we were from a university, were interested in learning more about serpent handlers, and would probably write an academic paper or article about them. Later, as the research progressed and we became more ambitious with our research plans, we explained that much of what we had read about serpent handling was untrue or misleading and that we wanted to write a book that gave a truer picture of serpent handling. We attended services, and when there were dinners on the church grounds we went to those too. After we became comfortable with the church services and knew some of the members we started conducting formal interviews in members' homes.

Because of our openness, we occasionally ran into uncomfortable situations. They often asked us about our own religious beliefs and our answers were not always well received. The assistant minister once asked Peggy what the Unitarian Universalist Church, which she attends, believes. She answered that Unitarians feel each person should seek God in her or his own way. The minister insisted that that view was wrong and that "what's right for me is right for you."

We think that we lost very little with our openness. However, there is no doubt that our experiences would have been different if we had approached the research differently. We attended church so regularly for such a long period that we came to be expected, and when we missed a service the minister would call on us to explain our absences. If we had not been open about our research, we would not have been able to schedule the interviews in members' homes in which we asked specific probing questions.

THE RESEARCH STAGES

We divided the research into two stages. The first stage consisted of establishing rapport and gathering basic information about the church. During the second stage we conducted formal interviews with members. We learned quickly the importance of dress and language. To be as unobtrusive as possible, we both dressed extremely conservatively. Neither of us wore jewelry and Kirk cut his hair shorter than usual while Peggy let hers grow longer. Peggy sewed clothes for herself that were decidedly not in fashion, but were in keeping with the very conservatively dressed women of the church.

We began learning a new vocabulary. Terms and expressions such as "anointment," "tongues," "shouting," and "carried away in the Lord" began to have meaning for us. We learned informally and often contextually through conversation and by listening to sermons and testimonials. The development of our understanding of the new language was gradual and probably was at its greatest depth when we were most submerged in the church and its culture. We avoided making conscious attempts to use newly learned phrases in conversation; rather, we allowed the new vocabulary to occur "naturally" in our conversations. For example, our spouses and friends had to tell us when we changed from saying, "He was bitten" to "He got bit," because the latter phrase came to "sound right" to us. We were conscious of the need to monitor our language. We simplified our language style and eliminated our use of profanity. We realized, for example, that one badly misplaced "damn" could destroy trust that we had built up over months of hard work. Some members, of course, would be more shocked than others. While we did not wish to annoy or alienate anyone, we were certain that it was impossible to avoid being unintentionally offensive to some. Monitoring our language was much easier during the first part of the research because then we were so conscious of everything we said. Later, as we became relaxed and friendly with many of the members, it was more difficult to guard against slipping into familiar speech patterns and using forbidden expletives.

When we initially returned to the church determined to begin serious research, we checked the location of the nearest hospital and brought a concealed snake bite kit with us to the services. Although we had been in no danger at the earlier services, we did not trust the snakes or what we then thought of as religious fanatics. As we attended more services, we began to forget the bite kit and the serpent handling became almost commonplace to us. As we gradually came to understand or assume the members' perspectives, the snakes seemed less threatening. When we became friends with members, some of our old fears returned, but in a different form. We no longer feared for ourselves but were apprehensive for some of our friends. As irrational as it may seem, we found ourselves looking at the serpent handlers from their perspective and asked ourselves, "Is that person really anointed?"[1]

We would be concerned if a member who had seemingly not been living "close to God" would take up a snake. We were among those who feared that a man who was said to be "young in the Lord" was so eager to take up a snake that he might handle one before God actually anointed him. We were caught up in the congregation's thrill if a member who had been praying and fasting to "get to take one up" was anointed. We came to understand, appreciate, and perhaps feel the frame of reference that says that serpent handling is a good thing.

After about eight weeks of attending services where we had observed some members tape-recording sermons, we asked and received permission from the minister to bring our tape recorders into the services. At first we recorded the entire two to three hour services, but later we omitted the songs and prayers, which were virtually incomprehensible anyway. We transcribed and catalogued these services for future analysis. We were even more cautious about taking photographs. They had told us of reporters who had used flash cameras and caused a sister to lose the anointment while she was handling a snake. We were six months into the research before we asked permission to bring a camera. Even then we never used a flash, as we tried to be as inconspicuous as possible. Once Kirk was leaning forward over the front row pew for a better camera angle and was so engrossed in his photography that he neglected to notice a rattlesnake being handled directly in front of him. The handler swung the snake up and it missed Kirk's nose by two inches. After that experience we moved back a couple of rows and Kirk began to use a more powerful camera lens.

EFFECTS ON OUR PERSONAL LIVES

The time spent with the serpent handlers had an impact on our personal lives and religious attitudes. Before the research we claimed liberal allegiance to ecumenicalism; nevertheless, we held a somewhat snobbish attitude toward fundamental Christian groups in general and regarded "fanatical groups" such as serpent handlers with amused disdain. Throughout the research, as we came to know the people and attended the services, we developed a genuine respect for the members, their beliefs, the style of service, and the religion.

We both had emotional experiences while attending this church. The prayers and acts of love and joy that members shared touched us. Twice the members of the church prayed for Peggy's two-year-old daughter, who underwent a series of heart operations during the time of the research. Once several members fasted for four days before praying for the child. Sometimes we wondered if, with our secular ways and rational thoughts, we were missing a peace and coming-to-terms-with-life that many of these members had. We often seemed to be spiritually far behind these loving ascetics and our own churches felt a little cold and impersonal.

BREAKING AWAY

Separating ourselves from the church was a painful process. Over the months we came to love many of the serpent handlers. Though we never seriously entertained the thought of accepting their belief system, we honestly enjoyed the services. However, when we had gathered our data and our research was ended, it was time to say goodbye. We had already started to disengage ourselves. Toward the end of the research, when we were interviewing people in their homes, we attended fewer and fewer of the services. By the time we completed the interviews we were attending service about once every three weeks.

After the interviews were completed, we returned to the church only twice during the next six-month period. It was difficult for us. When we went, the members asked where we had been and when we would come back. We missed the people, but we had run out of research and had no reason to continue to attend the services. We had no intention of converting to the belief system or to the style of life. It was a long drive to the little church and we had family, friends, and work that made demands on our time and energy. We were unprepared for how hard it was to say goodbye.

NOTE

1. An "anointed" person is given the power by God to handle a snake and, most believe, is therefore protected from harm.

Part II

Building Relationships

Getting In

RUTH HOROWITZ

In the early 1970s Ruth Horowitz conducted extensive field research among the Chicano residents of the 32nd Street neighborhood in Chicago. In the course of her research she became fascinated by the contradictions she observed in their behavior. She saw residents making great efforts to help one another, both financially and socially. At the same time, young men were shot on street corners while discussing ways of making peace among rival gangs. Residents demonstrated for better educational opportunities, yet the schools were discouraging and dangerous places. "The cultural life of this Chicago community," Horowitz wrote, "is organized around several pivotal themes: violence and convention, public life and private identity, honor and the American dream . . ."

To better understand this broad cultural pattern, Horowitz focused on teenagers as they interacted and developed identities in various social settings. She also examined the process through which young people make the transition from teenager to older community member. Her research highlighted the continual tension between the individualistic success ethic, as taught and expected in the schools and on the job, and the collective solidarity of the peer group.

Young people in this community carved out several distinctive lifestyles. Some young men were immersed in the social world of fighting gangs; others remained

This selection is adapted from Ruth Horowitz, *Honor and the American Dream: Culture and Identity in a Chicano Community,* copyright © 1983 by Rutgers, The State University. Reprinted by permission of Rutgers University Press. Also from Ruth Horowitz, "Remaining an Outsider: Membership to Research Rapport," *Journal of Contemporary Ethnography* 14, no. 4, pp. 413–423, copyright 1986 by Ruth Horowitz. Reprinted by permission of Sage Publications, Inc.

on the periphery, sometimes becoming involved in fights but generally only responding to what they perceived as insults rather than instigating incidents (a way to enhance a gang member's reputation). Other youth rigorously avoided the world of the streets and concentrated on getting an education or holding a job. But while their orientations to the street world were distinct, all the youth interacted with one another.

The young women moved in social worlds that were largely separate from those of the men. Most of them experienced tension in the realm of sexuality and motherhood. Only a few oriented their lives toward a work career. The others developed several strategies for resolving the dilemma between the importance of remaining a virgin and the need to give in to the sexual demands of a boyfriend.

Horowitz's research goals required that she spend a great deal of time with the teenage residents of 32nd Street as well as with families living in the community. She also observed residents in the schools, at political meetings, at dances and parties, and in the streets. For much of the time she hung out with the members of fighting gangs on street corners, in parks, and sometimes in their homes. She did not become a gang member; instead, she became accepted as a sort of reporter; some of the teenagers dubbed her "Lois Lane." But while her entry into the community and the lives of its residents was relatively easy, after a year she found that residents increasingly defined her in terms of local community expectations, creating problems for her as a "neutral" sociologist.

At times I have tended to romanticize my fieldwork experience. That tendency helped sustain me from 1971 through 1974 and brought me back to 32nd Street in 1977 to find out what had happened to the youths I first met in 1971. Attending local dances, parties, weddings, and cotillions was exciting, and sitting on a park bench or walking around the neighborhood talking and observing was an adventure. Many families made me feel at home by inviting me to family functions and letting me know that I was always welcome. They celebrated my birthday and spent long hours making *tamales,* which they knew were among my favorite foods. The romantic adventure image helped me overcome my fears and bear the tedium of dictating notes at two or three in the morning, often six nights a week.

The adventure was often overshadowed by the fears and drudgery of doing fieldwork alone. Some of the problems I encountered were typical of all fieldwork, others stemmed from the nature of the community I had chosen. Entering an unknown setting with no set status or identity, introducing myself to many people, and remembering names and their pseudonyms used in my notes was not easy. In the beginning I regarded every resident as critical to my research and thought that offending any one of them would compel me to leave the field.

Though I was fluent in Spanish, life in Spain, Mexico, and North Philadelphia had not prepared me for doing research. After moving to 32nd

Street in 1972, I quickly learned to distinguish between the sounds of gunfire and firecrackers and to block out the noise and music emanating from the pool hall below my apartment. However, I found the world of the streets sometimes a frightening place. Watching guns being passed through washroom windows to young women at public dances rattled me, particularly when we returned from the washroom to the dark, noisy dance floor, where a bystander could as easily have been shot as the intended victim.

Readers may wonder how a woman could possibly have spent time with gang members as they loitered on street corners and around park benches, and developed relationships that allowed her to gather sufficient and reliable data. I never tried to become a member of the community. The research role I developed through interaction with the youth varied from one group to another and was significantly influenced by some of my personal characteristics: I am Jewish, educated, small, fairly dark, a woman, dressed slightly sloppily but not *too* sloppily, and only a few years older than most of those whom I observed. These attributes did make a difference in how people appraised and evaluated me and my actions, and in the activities and thoughts to which I was privy. Careful observation of what kind of information was available to me and how different groups perceived and evaluated me allowed me to see not only what categories were important to each of the local groups and what someone in that role was permitted to see, do, and hear, but also how I should try to negotiate my identity in the field.

I had little choice but to acknowledge publicly the reasons for my presence on 32nd Street; not only do I differ in background from the 32nd Street residents but I had to violate many local expectations to gather the data I needed. While my appearance allowed me to blend into a youthful crowd, I sounded and looked sufficiently different so that most people realized immediately that I was not from the neighborhood. Much of the time it was advantageous to be an outsider and to be so regarded. For example, women do not spend time alone with male gangs as I did, especially without being affiliated with one of the gang's members. Moreover, as an outsider I could ask a lot of "stupid" questions—"Who are the guys in the black and red sweaters?" or "Why do you fight?" As anything but an acknowledged outsider I would have had a difficult time asking them.

While I spent some time with adults—teachers in several schools, families in their homes, and political activists in several community organizations—I spent most of my time with a variety of youth groups in the streets and at their other hangouts. Some of the youth were members of gangs who had and used guns; others were young women who frequently went out with these young men; others were much less involved in street life; and still others were college-bound.

Meeting young people was not as difficult as one might expect, given the public nature of much of their social life, particularly gang activity. In the first weeks of the project I chose to sit on a bench in a park where I saw many youth (aged 15 to 19) gathered from midafternoon until late at night. After several afternoons of sitting on a bench nearby, a male youth came over as I dropped a softball that had rolled toward me and said, "You can't catch" (which I acknowledged) and "You're not from the 'hood,' are you?" These were statements, not questions, by Gilberto, the Lions' president. I told him I wanted to write a book on Chicano youth. He told me that I should meet the "dudes" and took me over to shake hands with several of the members of the Lions gang. The park became my hangout every day after that, but it was several months, several bottles of Boone's Farm Strawberry Wine, and a number of rumors about my being a narcotics agent before many of the gang members would give me intimate information about their girlfriends, families, and feelings about themselves and the future. Some never did.

The facility with which I entered the community and eased into a fairly comfortable relationship with the Lions went to my head, and I nearly pushed my acceptance too far by not exercising a reasonable degree of caution. During my second month in the field, I heard about a gang peace meeting that was to take place on a Sunday afternoon at the park. All area gangs had been invited to attend. A perfect situation, I thought, a superb piece of data. On Sunday it was drizzling but I hurried down to 32nd Street. By 1:30 about 120 gang members had gathered under the porch of the park gym. Although I noticed that all the young women had disappeared from the park, I thought nothing of it.

The meeting began. A man in his late twenties started talking. I could not identify him as he was not wearing his "colors." He spoke for almost ten minutes about how the Chicano gangs had to stop fighting each other and instead get together for political purposes. Everyone listened attentively. Although I "saw" that several of them had guns, it did not register with me at the time.

Suddenly the speaker stopped and turned toward me, as did everyone else. My heart started doing triple time. He demanded, "Who are you?" I managed to say, "Hi! I'm Ruth and I'm writing a book on how the gangs are really together around here." Gilberto grabbed my arm, pulled me behind him, and said, "She's cool, she's been hanging with us." Another member of the Lions whispered to me to get out.

The gang member who challenged me at the peace conference was a Senior Greek. After the meeting I came back to the area where all the gangs were standing around. The speaker came toward me and invited me to join him and some other Senior Greeks at the corner tavern. They already had been drinking heavily. Frightened, but thinking only of the research opportunity, I followed them to the tavern. There they proceeded to tell me a story that sounded like the song "Officer Krupke" from *West Side Story:* They were "sick" and losers, the system was corrupt, and their parents had many problems. Over the next few years I got to know them much better, both how cruel and dangerous and how polite and thoughtful they could be.

My relationship with the male gang members evolved slowly and never was easy. Key elements of the identity we negotiated were my gender and the fact that I was an outsider. Being a woman both limited and expanded what I could see and do with the gang members. Remaining an outsider was essential. As a woman, I was not invited to attend fights or to go out looking for other gangs, but I was taken along to buy guns and was told afterwards about the fights, information that I would then verify with individual gang members and outside observers. I could talk to them about some aspects of their private lives, which they rarely discussed with other men. My lack of care with appearance, which both males and females continually remarked upon, allowed me to play down my sexual identity. However, I was very careful not to spend too much time alone with any one male and not to dance with them at the many parties and dances I attended.

The male gangs had a difficult time developing an identity for me that would allow them to be comfortable with a woman, as women do not hang around with men. However, as a woman I could do them little harm while they evaluated the situation; women can be harmful only when they are seen as controlling the situation. Gang members were the ones who could decide whether or not I could stay; I had made that option explicit. A man in a similar situation may have had a more difficult time, as his requests might be seen as a challenge. I later discovered that several weeks before I arrived a news photographer had had his camera taken from him and been told to leave.

The first dimension of my identity that I discovered they were constructing was as "a lady," which placed me in a respected but somewhat distant position from them. A "lady" implied that a woman was unobtainable sexually. One day when I was asked to accompany one of the members (age 15) to a corner grocery, we saw a young woman approaching and he said, "Here comes my girl." I had not met her and asked him if I should explain to her what I was doing. He replied that it was all right because she could see that I was a "lady." (His girl was not.) They began to treat me differently than the young women who sat in the park. They did not swear or discuss sex with a "lady," but did around some of the young women who spent time at the park. A man walked on the curb side with a "lady," helped to find her a chair, and took her arm to help her across an icy street; however, they did not do these things with most of the girls at the park. On several occasions a gang member would take my arm as we crossed an icy street, and when I dressed up for a fancy party, one of them rushed around to find me a comfortable chair. The youth frequently referred to their own mothers as "ladies." Here I was able to begin to discover the meaning of an important category to them and what they did in situations in which "ladies" are present.

However, "ladies" do not sit in the park and are not interested in gang members' lives. Social workers might be "ladies" who asked questions, but there were no outsider–social workers in the community, and the Lions discarded that category for me because I was at the park on evenings and weekends and did not try to make them do anything differently. Social workers worked from nine to five and told people what to do, they claimed. Finally, about four weeks after I arrived, and after examining the small notebook I carried with me, one of the gang members declared that I was like Lois Lane, the reporter (Superman's girlfriend). It was an identity that almost transcended gender. This provided them with the necessary identity with which I could ask about their activities and they could readily respond. Often they would seek me out to relay new stories of gang activities and, when someone wanted a story retold, to say, "Ask Ruth, she's been writing it all down."

Although the Lions began to treat me as a lady reporter, they still had misgivings as to what I was doing. Why would any outsider, particularly a woman, want to spend so much time with them? Both the researcher and the people who are being observed make sure the "data" are realistic by comparing them with their own ideas and experiences; the reliability of the data is checked by comparing what one is told with what is observed and with other accounts of the same events.

In the world of those whom I was observing, the police often asked questions. My behavior of asking questions and remaining in the background fit not only that of a reporter but also that of a "narc." A rumor that the narcotics squad was sending around a female agent gave rise to suspicion of my role. After I drank with them (fruit wines and beer) and watched them smoke marijuana and take acid without an arrest, that suspicion disappeared. Then they began to show me their weapons. One of the Lions showed me his radio, in which he had placed a small-caliber gun. He explained to me that he had seen guns put inside dictionaries on television, but he knew the police would be suspicious if they saw him carrying a book. When one of the Lions was arrested, not only did I make a small contribution to his bail but, as the only person over 21, I signed for him. Later I was asked and began to contribute small sums to the group's funds for beer and wine, which meant that they had decided that I was going to be around continuously. I had begun to notice that only those who were members of the group and always around contributed to the collective pot.

The outsider identity and somewhat marginal position of "lady reporter" allowed some closeness without being threatening as a woman who spent so much time with them asking what they often thought were dumb questions. This identity did not relegate me to lurking in the background, but allowed me to participate in many of the ongoing activities and was an indication of the limits of their interaction with adults in the wider society, their social skills, their categories of women, and the symbols they use to express the expected continuity of presence.

My identity as a lady reporter and the marginality that it implied had both advantages and disadvantages. Being a reporter allowed me to ask questions publicly about exciting events but not about family and personal experience. As a trusted, somewhat distant "lady," I had their respect. They would talk about their families in private; however, there were other things they would not discuss with or say in front of a "lady."

As a reporter I was allowed to check out accounts of fights by discussing them with individual members, the group, and older residents who had worked with gangs or had been members. From the very beginning, the gang members would talk about their fights and challenges by other gangs. Gathering data on fights and reputations was relatively easy, as it was seen that a reporter would be interested in their adventures.

Occasionally the subjects of school and work did arise naturally in the Lions' conversations; however, as a reporter and educated outsider I could probe these topics and probably extended them beyond their natural length in public discussions. School arose naturally as a topic of conversation when a particular event such as a fight, graduation, or suspension occurred. Work was a fairly common topic, as many of the Lions had worked, at least part time, from the age of 16. On other occasions, I would ask questions about school or work and, much of the time, a discussion would follow. As a recognized educated person (a reporter), I was asked questions about school and jobs.

Neither my identity as a reporter nor as a lady allowed me to obtain personal information concerning hopes, relationships with women, and families of the street youth. I was able to discover through conversations with former gang members that these were not topics discussed in public, and infrequently in private. Using the role of reporter was a failure; I tried to interview one of the gang members with a small portable tape recorder. He was so concerned about how he said things and "making a good story" that much of the material was so exaggerated and stilted that it was unusable. Only as a respected and trusted outsider was it possible for me to engage in such discussion.

The gang members could not discern what use personal information could be to me. However, they tried and failed to start rumors through me. In this way they gained confidence that I would not express their hopes and fears to others. They began to talk to me individually about themselves and the problems they had with their families and girlfriends.

Most of my discussions of family, girlfriends, and the future occurred when I would bump into one of the street-oriented males and he would ask for my advice about girlfriends, work, or school. Sometimes being slightly "high" encouraged the gang members to talk, but all questions had to be indirect. On one occasion I was talking to a Lion whose girlfriend had just told him that she was pregnant, when my reporter role got the best of me and I made the mistake of asking him why he had not used birth control in a tone that he took as an indictment of his behavior. With that comment, what had been a fascinating conversation about his intimate life, his fears of marriage and fatherhood, turned into a discussion of sports and fights. I had similar private conversations with many of the Lions and other street males, but some never felt close enough or trusted me enough to engage in such conversations.

On some occasions their evaluation of me as a "lady" proved an advantage. It allowed me to remain uninvolved. Being a "lady" limited opportunities to attend gang fights; when several gang members would take off in a car to shoot at some "enemies" I was rarely invited. My refusal to go even when asked was readily honored. Additionally, when I was asked to hide a gun, being "a lady," not a reporter, gave me the needed excuse to refuse. Except for gang fights, they rarely told me about illegal activities before they occurred, although they usually informed me afterwards. In their view, reporters did not know about stories until afterwards, and they were all aware that the wider society, of which I was a member, did not approve of much of their illegal behavior.

My identity as a "lady" did mean that swearing and public discussions of sexual exploits were limited. Watching how they reacted to me as a "lady," however, did tell me something about how they perceived that class of women. For example, one member was terribly embarrassed when I picked up a book he was reading and discovered that it was a graphic account of someone's sexual exploits. "Ruth, you shouldn't see that kind of thing," he said as he grabbed the book back. Through other measures, I was able to find out that they often discussed sex. When a male friend who was researching "rich kids" (which they found amusing) joined me at the park, they told him that they never talked about sex in front of me. There was no identity I could negotiate that would allow me to be privy to discussions of sex. I was unable to explore how they used public discussions of sexual relations and, therefore, was unable to explore the meaning of such discussions to group status and relationships.

*   *   *

Identities are not fixed, but are affirmed or changed continually. It was an advantage to be appraised as a lady and a reporter, as that identity allowed me to maintain a degree of distance and legitimacy as a woman among men. However, the longer I remained with the group, the more I became aware that some of the young men were attempting to redefine my identity as a potential girlfriend, making my sexual identity salient. After more than a year of using "lady reporter" as a key identity, some members began to flirt seriously and tried to ask me out. They claimed that my age (six to eight years older) did not constitute a barrier to starting a relationship. They were trying to replace my identity as a lady reporter with an identity that encompassed my potential as a sexual partner, regardless of my efforts to deemphasize my appearance and emphasize our age difference and my outsider status.

My failure to dress well initially acted as a deterrent to their appraising me in terms of my sexual identity. In contrast to my unpressed (but clean and unpatched) jeans, T-shirts or turtlenecks, and flat rubber-soled shoes or sandals, and my lack of make-up or a sophisticated hairstyle, the majority of young women on 32nd Street were much more concerned with appearance and dressed more neatly and fashionably in the latest style jeans or slacks (always well pressed), pretty blouses, and make-up. My lack of what they considered decent clothing and my inability to do anything with my hair were frequently a source of comment. One of the gang members teased me for two days when he noticed (immediately) that I had bought a new pair of shoes to replace the ones with holes, and several of the young women offered to lend me outfits when we discussed an upcoming dance. The young women frequently worried about my ability to "catch a man." While I dressed within the acceptable range, the remarks concerning my inability to dress well led me to see how important appearance was for both men and women. They also served, at first, to downplay my role as a sexual object.

Several of my actions may have encouraged the gang members' attempts to renegotiate my identity as an insider and sexual object. My move into a small apartment in the community was interpreted as a possible indication of community membership. Moreover, a friend from out of town came to visit, making the Lions aware that I might be attracted to some men, so they could begin to ask, "Why not us?" I had provided them with new information that they could interpret as indicating a need to change my identity.

While I was continually at the point of losing my lady reporter identity, I was not challenged all the time. I remained wary, making sure that other women were included on trips to the Lions' clubhouse and not dancing at parties. However, the attempts to renegotiate my identity began to limit my mobility and discussions with the gang and to reemphasize the importance of the wide gap between acceptable male and female roles and "ladies" and "chicks" that I had been observing.

As a lady reporter marginal to the community, I did not have to be treated as a sexual object and was free to spend time with men and ask questions. However, as an independent person I did not appear to be subordinate, which was threatening to their views of themselves as men who dominated women. Not only did I come and go as I wished, but I knew a lot about them. From their perspective, that gave me control. After fifteen months, their sexual teasing increased significantly; they commented about how good I looked, asked if I would go out with them, and several stated that I knew too much about them.

I did not know much more about their fighting, number of guns, or other illegal activities than many community residents. That was not what they were worried about. Rather, I knew too much about them as people—their problems, weaknesses, hopes, and fears. They needed one another and they knew that I knew that. I knew them too well and was aware that they were not all that they publicly claimed to be (tough warriors). They masked their intimacy and need for one another in order to be perceived publicly as tough. As soon as they began to see me as a potential sexual partner, my independence and possible control over them through intimate knowledge became problematic for them. As a woman, I should have been subordinate, but I was dominant through my independence and had potential power over them based on my intimate knowledge about them.

A sexual identity would have greatly impeded the research process. This culture creates strong parameters within which a female researcher would be very constrained as a community member. As the pressures increased to take a locally defined membership role, I was unable to negotiate a gender identity that would allow me to continue as a researcher. After eighteen months I had to stop spending so much time with the gangs and turned to the study of other youth groups in the community, seeing the gang members on occasion.

Earning a Place in the Hustler's World

ROBERT P. McNAMARA

Robert P. McNamara is an assistant professor of sociology at Furman University in Greenville, South Carolina. An expert on issues of deviance and social control, he has served as a consultant to state, federal, and private agencies on such topics as drug abuse, neighborhood safety, urban redevelopment, and policing. He is the author of several books dealing with deviance and crime in urban settings, including Crime Displacement: The Other Side of Prevention *and* Sex, Scams, and Street Life: The Sociology of New York City's Times Square.

In the early 1990s McNamara began what he describes as "a journey into the community of street hustlers in Times Square." In this context, hustling refers to male prostitution; the hustler is a male who engages in various sexual activities with other males for money, illegal drugs, or some other form of payment. McNamara was particularly interested in how hustlers develop a sense of cohesion. Through direct observation and open-ended, unstructured interviews, he sought to understand the culture of hustling and the interactions and relationships among the hustlers.

Recognizing that the Port Authority Bus Terminal served as a central meeting place for hustlers and their clients, he began hanging out there. For the better part of a year he spent three to five hours a day, two or three days a week, in coffee shops, fast-food restaurants, street corners, bars, and parks in the area around the bus terminal. He came to know many hustlers and had numerous conversations with them. He also spent a great deal of time simply observing their behavior, rituals, and activities.

This selection from McNamara's book The Times Square Hustler *describes how he gained access to the hustler population. Like other ethnographers who gain entry into the social worlds of people who engage in criminal or deviant behavior, McNamara found that his work was made easier by the hustlers' desire to tell their stories. People whose work or criminal careers make them social outcasts often develop an intense desire to explain themselves to those from the "respectable" world who care to listen. However, the ethnographer must prove that he or she is worthy of such confidences. How is this accomplished? This is the issue underlying McNamara's account of his experiences with the Times Square "boys."*

Gaining entry into hard-to-reach populations presents a host of problems for researchers. Often, the researcher must rely on informants to provide key information about the population as well as providing introductions to its members. Early on in my research, shopkeepers pointed out areas where a good deal of hustling takes place, offered opinions on the nature of the problem, and, in a few cases, introduced me to hustlers. My contacts with other researchers in the area and street people whom I had come to know were also helpful.

Through these networks, I was able to interview thirty-five hustlers. Because large segments of the population pride themselves on anonymity, I cannot make a claim about the representativeness of these interviews. However, I feel confident that what "the boys" have told me about the trade, the culture of hustling, and their lives has been accurate and consistent. When possible, I have verified the information through personal observation or by asking my informants or other hustlers for verification. These methods are obviously not without limitations, but they did serve to support the information provided by the boys. Nevertheless, it should be stressed that I am focusing on a select segment of the hustling population in New York City. My insights, assessments, and conclusions can only be applied to the hustlers in Times Square.

One of the most consistent questions people ask about this project, be they scholars or laypersons, is how I made initial contact with the boys. My first encounter with a hustler occurred after I had been in the field for about a month. I spent January making some preliminary observations as well as building a network to gain entrance into the population. I talked with people involved in the sex trade and the Times Square scene and attempted to learn more about the outreach programs in the area.

By February I felt I knew enough about the trade to begin interviewing hustlers. I encountered Eddie on the upper concourse of the Port Authority Bus Terminal. He was dressed in tight jeans, sneakers, and a hooded sweat shirt and was standing next to one of the doorways near the departure gates, a common pickup spot. Twice I saw him greet older men with a short conversation that ended with him shaking his head no. The men would depart and Eddie would remain, seemingly waiting for someone. He would make eye contact with a few passersby and in some cases quietly call out to them as they walked by. While this may appear to the casual observer as innocuous behavior, it led me to believe that Eddie was a hustler. I decided to approach him and determine if my initial assessment was correct: it was.

This was my first interview and I recorded it in my field notes immediately after it occurred. The verbal sparring was typical of the other encounters I had with hustlers who were not introduced to me.

MC: How's it goin'. I'm Bob.

E: I'm Eddie. How ya doin'.

MC: Listen I'm wondering if you could help me out, I'm writing a book about hustlers in Times Square. I was wondering if you knew anybody who hustled and would be willing to talk to me about it.

E: You writin' a book about hustlers? Here? How much?

MC: How much what?

E: How much you payin'?

MC: You don't understand, that's why I need your help. I don't have much money, but I could buy you lunch and we could talk about your experiences here.

E: You wanna what? Buy me lunch? What the hell am I gonna do with that? I can't spend that! You know my time is money, I can't be wastin' it talkin' to you or eatin' lunch.

MC: But you have to eat, right?

E: I'm not hungry.

MC: Okay, then how about I just stand here and hang out with you and ask you some questions until a trick comes along and then you leave?

E: If you stand around here, no tricks will come cause they'll think I'm talkin' to you.

MC: All right, what if you introduced me to some of your friends who hustle who aren't working now. You tell them what I'm doing and that I can't pay cash and basically say I'm okay. Then when you do have time and you are hungry, we can talk some more. That way you don't have to worry about losing money now and you can help out one of your friends who is hungry and who isn't hustling today.

E: So what do I get out of it?

MC: What you get out of it is that you help out one of your friends, you help me, and then the next time I see you, you can help yourself. You aren't always hustling. You have to eat at some point, so let me buy you lunch and all we're going to do is talk. If I ask you something you don't want to answer, then don't. So we would be helping each other and your friends. And if you and I get along, maybe you can introduce me to more of your friends or maybe you and I can hang out sometime. But right now, it doesn't cost you anything and all I want to do is meet other hustlers who aren't working so I can talk to them. After you introduce me and tell them what's up, you're done.

E: And all you want to do is talk? Nothin' else? And you can't pay? Oh, lord, what do I look like, some sort of social worker?

MC: You look like a guy who's smart enough to see what this is about and you are also smart enough to see that this could work out for everybody. You help your friends out and yourself at the same time. So how about it?

E: Okay, but I want to talk to you first. If you writin' a book I want my name in it. But I'm only gonna give you ten minutes. If I like you, I'll help you, but if I don't, I ain't doin' shit. Come on, you can buy me a slice over at that pizza shop.

That interview with Eddie lasted forty-five minutes. From that point on, he introduced me to many of his friends. Once he started talking he never stopped, but getting him to talk to me initially was a crucial step.

Many of my colleagues (and even some of the boys) have expressed surprise at how quickly and thoroughly I was able to gain access to this population. There were three primary reasons for my success. One of the things that helped establish my position in the culture was my willingness to deal with the same adversities the boys faced. They told me I earned their respect because, despite the freezing cold of winter or the sweltering heat of summer, I "hung out" and suffered from the elements along with them.

Moreover, unlike others in their lives, I was interested in what they had to say, did not pass judgment on them or their opinions, and was straightforward from the time of my initial contact with them. This, according to the boys, earned their respect. Prince told me:

> You never dissed [show a lack of respect] us. You always straight up and you listen. You okay man, for a white boy, you okay. Like I never get to tell nobody how I feel about shit, you understand? Things like life and shit. But you, I know you interested in me and what I gots to say, I like that. And most of these other guys like that too. That's why you was accepted so fast. Like I said, you okay as far as I'm

concerned. How many people you know will come out here, ask us how we doin', buy us lunch, ask us if we okay and then give us your phone number and say call if we need anything? You ain't really no researcher as far as I'm concerned, you a friend of ours.

While this is indeed speculation on my part, and based largely on my own beliefs and assessment, I think my immersion into the environment was successful in part because I went to the hustlers in their setting instead of having them come to me in mine. I also felt I could not, in good faith, represent myself to be something I was not. The trust that I engendered was tenuous in some instances, but I believe it may have been based on my fulfillment of any promises I made. For example, if I talked to someone on the condition that I would buy him lunch in return or meet him on a certain day to help him with welfare benefits, I felt obliged to show up as promised or else I should not have agreed to help in the first place. I believe they knew this and, as time progressed, they began to trust me and tell me more about themselves. This research approach granted me entrance into a hidden population in Times Square that few researchers have explored in any detail.

I was also very concerned about confidentiality and protecting the hustlers' identities. I applied for, and received, a Certificate of Confidentiality from the United States Department of Health and Human Services. This provided legal protection for my sources. I made a point of explaining what this document was and how it maintained their anonymity. I also took the added precaution of asking them what they wanted to be called rather than simply using their street names. In some cases, they said it did not matter, but I wanted to be clear about what I was doing and why. These boys appeared indifferent and said their street names could be used. Nonetheless, as an added precaution, I use fictitious names for these individuals.

I also told the boys that I would bring them some of my field notes to read if they were so inclined. Later, I explained, I would also bring the completed chapters along so that they could give me their comments and offer any suggestions or clarifications that they felt were needed. This went a long way toward enhancing my credibility and standing in the community. My offer to share the contents of my work was perceived as an honest attempt to understand their world and learn from them, not to simply extract the information and depart, never to be heard from again.

A second factor in my success with the boys involved my passing a series of tests. For instance, a hustler would share a piece of information with me, make me promise it was to be held in the strictest of confidence, and then wait to see if I mentioned it to anyone else. When I did not, he would tell others that I was trustworthy. Other tests determined if I would uphold my end of an arrangement. Early on, I had established an agreement with the boys that I could not give them cash but would be willing to buy them lunch, cigarettes, or other incidentals in exchange for their time and insight. This was done to offset the income they would forgo by talking to me.

As they came to know and trust me, this issue became moot, and the boys would freely seek me out to tell me the latest news of their lives or what had happened since our last meeting. Our interaction became less an exchange and more a social relationship. I still purchased incidentals or lunch for them, but I would usually bring the subject up by asking a boy if he had eaten that day.

To test my resolve as well as their ability to "work" me, some hustlers would occasionally ask for a dollar or two to buy groceries for their family. I would remind them of our understanding, and, in turn, they would try to play on my sympathies. One parrying tactic I used was to offer to buy groceries for them and to have them take me to meet their "incredibly beautiful but hungry baby."

The point in all the tests or attempted scams was to determine whether I would make exceptions to our agreement. If I wavered even once, a precedent would be set and a deluge of requests might follow. Moreover, my standing in the community would be damaged: I could be "played." Knowing this, I remained steadfast in my position. As it turns out, this was the correct response. Within a short time, perhaps three or four months into the project, the tests had all but stopped. Occasionally a hustler reintroduced one, but it was usually a playful attempt, performed more as a joke coupled with a reminder of how the hustlers had "tested" me in the past. . . .

Despite my acceptance into the culture, I encountered difficulty from some hustlers who did not believe what they had heard about me. In an effort to remedy this, I often carried economy-sized packs of chewing gum, which I offered to those I knew and those I had just met. It was a great icebreaker and allowed me to inform them that I was simply trying to write about their lives. As time went on, my acquaintance with other hustlers served as a legitimizing mechanism. That is, my credibility was enhanced by having already talked to people the skeptics knew.

An obvious potential problem in working with this population was my personal safety. While I was accepted by most hustlers, who evinced a sense of responsibility for my safety, I could not rely on them completely in the event of trouble. One precautionary strategy that I adopted was to call home on an hourly basis. I also sent letters to the Port Authority Police and the mayor's Office of Midtown Enforcement explaining who I was and that I was conducting social science research in the area. I also explained that as a security precaution I would be checking in periodically at home and that if anything went wrong, my wife would contact their office with my description and last known location.

Whenever I arrived in Times Square, I would check in and tell my wife where I was and where I would be going during the next hour. An hour or so later, I would call and tell her where I was going next. If I did not check in within a two hour period, she was to call the police. I gave myself a two hour cushion in the event I could not easily break away to call, such as during a very personal or emotional interview with one of the boys. This was not a strategy without limitations and there were a few instances where I came extremely close to violating the two hour limit. Fortunately, my wife understood the difficulties of field research and remained calm. Interestingly, my informants understood my purpose in checking in and even reminded me to "go check in" on a few occasions. They would then explain my brief absence to others who might not know why I left.

Another problem that I confronted was my role in the culture. In deviant populations, members must always keep a wary eye out for the police, particularly undercover officers. This is especially true in Times Square, where the Port Authority Police as well as the New York City Police Department have escalated their undercover "sting" operations. As a result, strangers are given a great deal of scrutiny.

One problem in researching this population is that there are very few roles that an adult male can play. Essentially, one is perceived as either a client, a police officer, a commuter or "suit," or in some cases, an older hustler. Since I purposely avoided dressing like a "fly Puerto Rican" [hip, in style] the latter possibility was quickly eliminated. The role of researcher was not at all defined.

Many of the boys stated that they initially thought I was a police officer. They sensed something about my presentation of self, or in their words, I "smelled like a cop." There may be some accuracy to this assessment since I had six years experience as a security officer as well as some law enforcement training. In many ways, I may have indeed "smelled" like a police officer. Others thought I was a client, especially when they saw me talking to many different hustlers.

I had a few encounters in which one hustler propositioned me in front of another, which set off a round of arguments and angry threats. This occurred for two primary reasons. One was the aforementioned sense of responsibility my informants felt for my safety, while the other reason has to do with the normative system that regulates the boys' behavior. In either case, my role was not at all clear. Eventually, the word spread that I was writing a book about hustlers in Times Square and my place in the neighborhood became understood and accepted.

This role was carefully constructed for the reasons I just outlined. I needed to maintain a sense of distinction and separation so that others who did not know me would be able to understand who I was without cause for concern. I wanted to be part of the culture, but at the same time I needed a certain objective distance in order for my presence to be understood as well as to prevent my "going native." . . .

How I dressed played a very important role, especially early in the course of the project. While some researchers might find themselves thinking about how to dress like the natives lest they be identified as outsiders, I had the somewhat difficult task of trying to dress differently. This was especially important since I did not want to be mistaken for an undercover police officer. Had I tried to dress like a hustler, I would have certainly been identified as a police officer, and if I dressed as I normally did, I would also be identified as one. The boys felt that white men, especially white men in their early to late thirties, who wore untucked tennis shirts and various sports-related clothing such as National Football League (NFL) jackets or hats, had various bulges around the waistband, and spent a lot of time standing around watching people, were cops. This made it very difficult to gain entry into the population. Here again, my informants played a key role. After I got to know them, they legitimized my presence by introducing me to other hustlers.

Relations of the Road

DOUGLAS HARPER

Douglas Harper has spent years studying the lives of people on urban skid rows and in hobo jungles. In his book Good Company *he discusses his experiences as a participant observer in the hobo's world. He contrasts the life of tramps who ride freight trains and find casual labor in the cities and western fruit farms with the more sedentary, yet also more self-destructive, life of skid-row bums.*

Photographs were an important part of the material Harper collected while living with the tramps. They became "a visual inventory of typical behavior in typical spaces—for this group." But as the following account illustrates, the photos could not be allowed to intrude on his participation in the tramp life.

Also important to Harper's research was his friendship with a longtime tramp, Carl, who became his companion on the journey described in Good Company. *Carl educated the sociologist-photographer, explaining how to survive on the road, showing him how to interact with other tramps, and eventually telling him his own story. In fact, the growing friendship between Harper and Carl was typical of how tramps come together on the road, share each other's lives for a time, and then part company.*

Of course, in order to conduct his research Harper had to learn how to locate trains and board them without being driven out of the yards. Freight trains are dangerous and difficult to ride, and riding them is illegal. Mastering the trains requires resourcefulness, cunning, persistence, and intelligence. For the tramp, the trains are a proving ground. For Harper, too, there was a process of initiation, a period in which he felt too intimidated to ride the trains, and eventually a feeling of confidence and even pleasure as he grew to understand the hobo's life. An especially striking aspect of this selection is the mixture of fear and joy he experienced as he climbed onto a train and reentered the tramp world.

I'd been waiting for a train a year before in the same yard heading in the same direction but nothing seemed particularly familiar. The Minneapolis Burlington Northern yards stretch northwest from under the University and they go on for miles; ten, fifteen, twenty tracks wide; spurs heading north, spurs heading east; and somewhere in the maze a main line that carries the hotshot out of Chicago through Minneapolis to the west. I stood in the shadows of huge grain elevators, out of sight of the control tower, and I waited for a train due at midnight.

I'd been in the yards a couple of days, peeking around, asking questions and making plans. Every time I've come back to the freights I've had to cross an emotional hurdle—they seem too big, too fast, too dangerous, and too illegal—and I get used to the idea by spending a few days in the yards, testing the waters. If the brakemen aren't busy they'll answer a carefully worded question. If there are railroad police around it's better to encounter them just hanging around; no gear and no suspicious behavior. Then you choose the day: Tomorrow you'll ride; tonight you'll party and pack your gear and tomorrow you'll be back on the road. Then when you walk past the No Trespassing signs into the yard your traveling clothes and your gear mark you clearly. You enter a world that has its own rules and few second chances, and you'd better know what you're up to.

I was shifting back into a tramp world for the fourth or fifth time. I'd made cross-country trips on freights and I'd spent some weeks the winter before living on Boston's skid row. While my purpose was to describe a tramp way of life, it was only part of the reason I'd go back again and again. The taste of camp coffee and the view from a flatcar on a slow ride through the Rockies were magnets that pulled hard indeed. This time I felt my gear in order and plans set. The Chicago hotshot would carry me across the Dakotas, Montana, and the Rockies. As much as I had a destination it was Wenatchee, Washington, for I knew it to be the center of the apple country and a junction of major rail lines. I knew the jungles in Wenatchee and I knew that there would be tramps there to steer me to a job. The Chicago hotshot, with the right connections, should get me to Wenatchee in no more than a couple of days. I mulled it over and relaxed. It seemed manageable, and it seemed in grasp.

After perhaps half an hour the activity increased in the yard. Strings of boxcars were pushed up and down the parallel tracks, shuffled into boxcars, flatcars, gondolas, and piggybacks that were then pushed uncoupled over the hump. The humped cars slammed into pieces of trains down one of the fifteen or twenty tracks that led away from the small hill. It was all controlled by invisible workers in a control tower that loomed above. The cars were shuffled and reshuffled; a few empties or badorders set off and pushed aside; a string of piggybacks or gondolas pushed into place— it went on and on like a carefully rehearsed play. I watched idly until I noticed a long string of empty grain cars and flatcars moving into place. I guessed that the grain cars would be going west, probably to Minot or Havre, and that the flats would go on to the lumbering country in the Rockies. As the train stretched out further and further I decided to find out.

I picked my way across the yard. It is with utmost care that one climbs over the couplings of boxcars for it is impossible to know when a car or engine will slam into it, compressing the long shaft on which the coupling is mounted and setting the car into a slow roll. The proper procedure is to throw one's gear over the couplings, then to climb across the space on the ladders and the braces on the car itself. It is quickly apparent in a freight yard that the scale is unhuman—a small jolt to a freight car or a small compression of a coupling is enough to fling a person from the car and if you fall off climbing over you'll be run over or dragged down the yard. I moved over the couplings, first with hesitancy and then with more confidence as I found my "rail legs."

I found the longest section of train and began walking its length. I walked down the narrow canyon between the cars and came upon a tramp crouched near the door of the first empty boxcar. He did not see me coming and displeasure crossed his face when I suddenly appeared. He smelled of booze, sweat, and urine and his work uniform looked like he'd slept in it for a week. His face was scarred and unshaven. He had some gear back in the boxcar; I asked him where he was headed. It was clear he wanted nothing to do with me but he answered that he was going west to pick apples. I told him that I too was going to Wenatchee to pick apples, but he answered, not a little sarcastically, that there wasn't any good work in *Wenatchee,* you had to go north, up the Okanagan to a place like Oroville. Before I could ask him where that was he'd slunk back to the corner of his car. I walked on to find my own.

I was nearly to the end of the train before I found another empty boxcar. It was old and battered, without wooden liners on the walls that would cool and quiet the ride. The wheels were mounted in old-style bearings that make an empty car jump and skitter, and the floor was covered with strapping iron and sawdust. I did not like the car but it was the only inside ride on the train. I checked to see if it was a badorder on its way to a repair yard before I threw my gear in the door.

I found some cardboard sheets to make a mattress and pushed some of the litter out of the car. A brakeman stuck his head in the door and startled me with a greeting. He told me the train was due out on the highline—the old Great Northern tracks—as soon as it got its power. It would make the 500-mile run to Minot before breaking up and it should get me there a few hours before the hotshot which was due at midnight, so I'd be able to catch a few hours sleep before continuing on. Then our conversation should have been over but he lingered. He told me he'd tramped all over the west when he was younger and he always tried to help a man out "as long as they looked like they knew what they were doing." It was all going down hill, he said; the tramps were bums and there were hippies on the trains always getting into trouble. You don't mind a rider, he repeated, if they know what they're doing. But the hippie will lie around in the open smoking dope as though it's a picnic, and then they'll get hurt and sue the railroad. He shook his head to show his disgust, and walked away.

As the engine jockeyed into position at the front of the train my car was slammed backward and forward. I worked quickly to peg the doors open with old brake linings and railroad spikes I found lying around the yard. It is an important job, for if the doors jolt shut there is no way to open them from the inside. As I worked, a yard engine lumbered by, sounding like it was overrevving with the pent-up power of huge diesel engines pushing it oh so slowly by. Two green Burlington Northern engines, attached back to back, idled alongside and past my boxcar. I caught sight of the engineer and our eyes met briefly but his expression did not change. Just a minute later the air hissed down the brakelines and the highball whistle blew. I was filled with a lonely sort of expectancy—an intense desire to be under way. Then the engineer snapped the throttle back, the jolt crashed down the train and the trip began.

As the train gained speed the memories came flooding back. The noise and movement are soon more than I've experienced. Nothing can be so loud! Nothing can throw me about with such abandon! The car, sprung for hundreds of tons, carries me as a tiny piece of flotsam bouncing, banging, swaying. The car rocks from side to side and I think of empty boxcars tipping and taking whole freight trains with them. You don't live through those, say the tramps. The car bangs so hard on road crossings I hold my mouth open to keep my teeth from cracking together. I try to sit and my body leaps off the floor and my sleeping bag skitters away. Slack creeps into the mile-long train and as the car suddenly snaps ahead I find my body accomplishing the anatomical feat of moving three directions at once. I stand with my legs spread for balance, holding a wall to keep from pitching over, bending my knees to take up the shock of the ride. The train highballs and the tracks are bad and my car rides worse than any I remember. Or perhaps it just seems this way every time I go back. The eight hours ahead seem interminable but the train does not slow to ease my aches.

I spend the hours standing by the doors. When the tracks parallel a highway I catch a glimpse of car travelers safely encapsulated. Sometimes they wave but more often they look away and shield their children from the sight of me. An outlaw so soon! I laugh aloud but I cannot hear myself above the din of the train. I am captured by the absurdity. I run back and forth through the car; leap, play, dash about. The train moves on its own; I'm but a small grain attached. With all the swirling grit my trip is cleaner by far than those on the highway for there is no windshield constricting my view and no billboard to funnel my attention. I feel the land, standing quite near, and it becomes very much a part of my trip.

I pass through time as the train slices through pink and avocado subdivisions of towns; through belts of older, taller, and more muted houses; and finally through stone-facaded mainstreets. The train depots had been the kernels from which these towns grew, but now only an old trainman stands on the platform and waves as the freight highballs through.

We pass for an hour through an area dotted with lakes before entering the Red River valley. The transformation is quick and complete. Fields of sunflowers stretch to the horizon; then come quarter section after quarter section of corn with farm buildings and houses tucked into small tree-filled corners and straight and regular roads tying it all together.

Well into the evening the train slowed for the first time to a 15-mile-an-hour idle through the Fargo/Moorhead yards and I watched ten or twelve tramps waiting to board. I stood in the door to claim my space and they stayed away from my car. I was glad to be left alone when the train pulled into the North Dakota prairie.

As the sun set, the train turned due west. I looked around the edge of the door and watched the mile-long train bore directly into the orange sun on the horizon. It got dark fast and I became depressed, feeling quite alone. I was nearly overcome with tiredness before I crawled into my sleeping bag and fought my way to sleep in the lurching, rocking, and screeching freight car.

*   *   *

The next days brought a slow ride on bull locals through the Dakotas, Montana, Idaho, and Wahsington. I'd missed a connection or the brakeman had lied to me, but either way I was far from the fast trains of the highline. The tramp I'd met in Minneapolis, sour from his three-week drunk, broke and hungry, had become my companion. I had a loaf of bread made into peanut butter and jelly sandwiches, and even though it became a sticky oozing mess in the heat of a Montana August, it kept us going for a couple of days. The tramp made it clear that he would have preferred beans. As he sobered up, our relationship quietly began.

"You know," he said once after we had been together for a couple of days, "you can't trust everybody you meet. I can see it in your manner. You're too open, you're—what's the word—too naive."

"That may be, but you left your gear with me plenty of times. I could've taken off with it."

"You aren't goin' nowhere. Got too much shit of your own. Anyway, you don't know enough to be afraid of. This life ain't no bed of roses. I've lost too much gear not to know that. You know how much this sleeping bag cost me? That's forty-five dollars right there. It's what they call a Red Fox. It's got that new-fangled material in it."

"It's good to travel with a sleeping bag," I said.

"Yeah, *if* you can keep it. You know the people you work with, they're bigger thieves than anybody. And then there are guys just to rob you, to git your money and your gear."

"Are these regular tramps you're talking about?"

"Well, they travel the country like your regular tramps, but they ain't no tramps. We call them jackrollers. And once in a while you'll get young kids that'll do the same thing. You can't trust anybody, and I ain't kidding. Where we're headed, up there north of Wenatchee, that's country you got to be careful of. Ain't too bad goin' in, but comin' out, after the harvest, then you got to be careful. What I always do is make my wages and ride out of there payin'. Let that freight go all alone. And I seldom drink on the freight—I'll take it somewhere else.

"You got to understand something—you're just a tramp, and nobody wants nothun' to do with you unless it's your money or your work. The cops are no different. I got busted for drunk in Spokane last year, hell, I hadn't seen a bottle for three days! An' you always leave jail with clean pockets. But the worst ones are the jackrollers. See this one?" The tramp pointed to a scar that led from the corner of his left eye down along his nose and across his lips. "That happened in Minneapolis. All they got off me that time was four dollars in cash and ten dollars' worth of groceries."

"Were you drunk?"

"Hell, no, I was asleep. Woke up in the Hennepin County Hospital; they hit me in the face. Just missed my eye."

"Where were you staying?"

"I was *heading* west."

"Were you in a freight yard? In a boxcar?"

"Hell, no, I was out in the weeds. It's easy to find a man in a boxcar. You're a sitting duck in a boxcar. But they follow you out to the weeds, too. They watch, they watch for you and follow you out. *You'll* get it if you're not careful. I won't lay down in that boxcar, either, unless it's moving. And when that train is moving I got one eye open and I'm on my feet the moment he stops . . .

"You'll see, it's all changing. Used to be all you'd find on this road was the tramp, and this time of year it would be the fruit tramp, what we call the apple knocker. But nowadays they're not all tramps. Seattle is so damn screwed up they'll come out of there to find work. And they're starting to get Mexicans in some places. Your real tramps won't associate with them. But most of the Mexicans stay down south, thinnin' beets, that's good work for them. Stoop labor, that's what they like. And the government's gettin' on a lot of camps where you'd live, closing them up. They're filthy places. But then there is no place for a man to stay. You have to carry a tent. I know some guys that do it, carry a tent. Lightweight tents. And sometimes you'll build a shack. One guy will work days, the other nights. That way there'll always be somebody around to watch the stuff. But you got to be careful, really careful. I camped with a man and a woman last year and they stole what I had. Panasonic radio, worth forty dollars. AM/FM radio. Twelve bucks' worth of groceries. And my bag with my change of clothes in it. But I know who they are and sooner or later I'll get them. You can't escape on this road—everybody knows you after a while . . ."

The tramp and I spent a month together, winding our way across the west to the apple harvest in northern Washington State. We jungled together with other tramps in the harvest town and were eventually hired out to pick apples. We met a tramp he'd known for years and he taught me the proper tramp etiquette. We'd "buddied-up," as tramps typically do—by sharing food, supplies, time, and miles—but Carl taught me that a tramp makes his own decisions and eventually moves on alone. He accepted my food because he was down and out, but he knew I was not a regular and he was suspicious of what he'd have to pay. During our first days together he realized I did not really know what to expect from him and he warned: "Some people on this road are helpless. When you start helpin' it's just like having a son . . . They don't know where it stops! You got to support them—take care of them—you got to provide the hand and I won't do that. If a fella is on this road and he can't learn— then to hell with him." Later he added: "When you get your job, don't depend on nobody else. If you want to leave, then leave! That's it—a lot of these guys say, 'If you quit, let me know and I'll quit with you.' I say bullshit. Before you know it you'll have run out of places to work."

I understood even less, I realized very early, about relationships I observed among other tramps. As I watched an elaborate exchange of coffee, food, and clothes between Blackie and Carl I noted what I thought to be a wonderful generosity that existed on the road. Later I learned that Blackie was a sonofabitch trying to get Carl indebted for future business. Yet later when we jungled before the harvest there were few supplies anywhere and everything a tramp had became common property. I slowly and awkwardly came to understand these events and to participate in them in a way that could be called normal by those in the life.

But even though Carl tried to make our relationship typical, it never was. At first he taught me how to make it on the road and ignored most of my questions. Something changed the chemistry between us and he stepped out of his normal role to tell me about his childhood, his parents, and his life before hitting the road. I had learned not to expect such self-revelations, and I think Carl sensed as well that they constituted transgressions of the normal tramp way. At the end he distanced himself again and made it clear that the things we had been discussing were off limits and that when it came time to leave he would be on his way alone.

My sociological eye observed all this, yet my emotional character acted on its own. In becoming committed to Carl the individual (as opposed to Carl the tramp) I offered unwanted advice and rather unconsciously set out to reform my buddy. Carl humored me—I told him he ought to put a part of his stash in the bank before he started a binge, and he said: "I do—bartender's bank!" Or, just after telling me he expected to buy a cabin in Montana and I said I'd like that too, he replied: "That's what I want to get away from . . . neighbors." But finally, I began to feel a grudging respect and a partial acceptance. Just before I left he said: "I've noticed you change. You've learned that you can make it on the road—now if something overloads it'll always be in the back of your mind. You watch yourself—you'll be reverting back."

But as I became more like Carl in manner and behavior, and perhaps more hardened by the experiences we shared, I could not leave my other values behind. When he opened up to me I responded with friendship (a category from my life, not his). When he distanced himself I felt rebuffed, and I felt a great loss at the end of our time together. I never really learned to experience the world as a tramp and I knew that unless I moved completely into that life my values would probably remain in the world of relationships and commitments.

*   *   *

As I involved myself more I had to reassess my purpose and methods. I could have continued as I had begun and produced a photographic study from the viewpoint of an outsider, but as I felt myself pulled into the life, my photographic activity changed very much. On the trip I have described I carried a Leica and a single lens—a small, unobtrusive and quiet camera. I made few photographs during my time with Carl. I introduced myself as a writer and photographer and he did not seem to mind my taking pictures until we encountered people he'd known for a long time; then he made it clear that to carry on would be out of the question. Some of the photographs I did make, however, show how the camera may describe the relation between "researcher" and "informant." The image that communicates this best is of Carl handing me a piece of toast. The toast was made at my request. The fire was the first we'd made in days. A long trip was nearly completed and our relationship had the quality of those in which important events have been shared. I am satisfied with the photograph for it describes both an important activity and the nature of our relationship. The photographs I did not take, of Boston Blackie, One-Eyed Jack, and the jungles along the way testify by their absence to the same issue. The relationship between the photographer and subject in a fieldwork experience is very complicated, but for me the rights and desires of the individuals we choose as subjects are more important than a final purpose that would justify making images when they would not be welcomed. The camera must sometimes be left behind.

Photo courtesy of Douglas Harper.

Photo courtesy of Douglas Harper.

Part III

Maintaining Objectivity

Doing Research
in Cornerville

WILLIAM F. WHYTE

William Foote Whyte's study of life in an Italian-American slum has become a classic of the sociological literature. Whyte conducted his research in "Cornerville," a slum district of a large East Coast city, for three and a half years. During much of that time he lived with an Italian family, not only to obtain an intimate view of family life but also to establish contacts with the wider community. He learned Italian, joined in community activities such as bowling and baseball, and gained the confidence and friendship of the residents of Cornerville.

Whyte's analysis of Cornerville focused on the structure and leadership of informal groups of "corner boys" and their relations with other groups within the community, especially political organizations, racketeering organizations, and the police. The results of his research were published in his famous book Street Corner Society.

In this selection Whyte describes how he obtained a sponsor, Doc, who introduced him to all the individuals and groups he wished to study. As Whyte puts it, this situation was "perfect." Despite his good fortune in meeting Doc, however, Whyte encountered a number of obstacles in the course of his research. In discussing his experiences he points out that "the researcher, like his informants, is a social animal." If researchers live for an extended period in the community they are studying, their personal life is inextricably mixed with their research. Each researcher deals with this issue somewhat differently, but each must deal with it in some way.

In the following pages Whyte describes how he merged his personal life with that of his friends and neighbors, but in this introduction it is worth mentioning that his integration into the life of the community had some intriguing consequences. In the fall of 1937 the position of mayor of Eastern City was up for election. Whyte joined the campaign of one of the candidates, running errands and doing odd jobs such as nailing up posters in various parts of the district. On election day he voted and then reported for duty at the campaign headquarters. As the voting proceeded, it became evident that the opposition candidate was stealing the election. The solution: All the supporters of Whyte's candidate were to go out and vote again— several times.

Eventually Whyte learned that to be accepted by the people in a community it is not necessary to do everything just the way they do it. But as is true for many researchers in the field, it was a lesson learned the hard way.

When I began my work, I had had no training in sociology or anthropology. At the time I was sitting in on a course in slums and housing in the Sociology Department at Harvard. As a term project I took on a study of one block in Cornerville. To legitimize this effort, I got in touch with a private agency that concerned itself in housing matters and offered to turn over to them the results of my survey. With that backing, I began knocking on doors, looking into flats, and talking to the tenants about the living conditions. This brought me into contact with Cornerville people, but it would be hard now to devise a more inappropriate way of beginning a study such as I was eventually to make.

Shortly thereafter I met a young economics instructor at Harvard who impressed me with his self-assurance and his knowledge of Eastern City. He had once been attached to a settlement house, and he talked glibly about his associations with the tough young men and women of the district. He also described how he would occasionally drop in on some drinking place in the area and strike up an acquaintance with a girl, buy her a drink, and then encourage her to tell him her life-story. He claimed that the women so encountered were appreciative of this opportunity and that it involved no further obligation.

This approach seemed at least as plausible as anything I had been able to think of. I resolved to try it out. I picked on the Regal Hotel, which was on the edge of Cornerville. With some trepidation I climbed the stairs to the bar and entertainment area and looked around. There I encountered a situation for which my adviser had not prepared me. There were women present all right, but none of them was alone. Some were there in couples, and there were two or three pairs of women together. I pondered this situation briefly. I had little confidence in my skill at picking up one female, and it seemed inadvisable to tackle two at the same time.

Still, I was determined not to admit defeat without a struggle. I looked around me again and now noticed a threesome: one man and two women. It occurred to me that here was a maldistribution of females which I might be able to rectify. I approached the group and opened with something like this: "Pardon me. Would you mind if I joined you?" There was a moment of silence while the man stared at me. He then offered to throw me downstairs. I assured him that this would not be necessary and demonstrated as much by walking right out of there without any assistance.

For my next effort I sought out the local settlement houses. They were open to the public. You could walk right into them, and—though I would not have phrased it this way at the time—they were manned by middle-class people like myself. I realized even then that to study Cornerville I would have to go well beyond the settlement house, but perhaps the social workers could help me to get started.

It was at the settlement house that I met Doc. I had talked to a number of the social workers about my plans and hopes to get acquainted with the people and study the district. They listened with varying degrees of interest. If they had suggestions to make, I have forgotten them now except for one. Somehow, in spite of the vagueness of my own explanations, the head of girls' work in the Norton Street House understood what I needed. She began describing Doc to me. He was, she said, a very intelligent and talented person who had at one time been fairly active in the house but had dropped out, so that he hardly ever came in any more. Perhaps he could understand what I wanted, and he must have the contacts that I needed. She said she frequently encountered him as she walked to and from the house and sometimes stopped to chat with him. If I wished, she would make an appointment for me to see him in the house one evening. This at last seemed right. I jumped at the chance. As I came into the district that evening, it was with a feeling that here I had my big chance to get started. Somehow Doc must accept me and be willing to work with me.

The social worker showed us into her office and then left so that we could talk. Doc waited quietly for me to begin, as he sank down into a chair. I found him a man of medium height and spare build. His hair was a light brown, quite a contrast to the more typical black Italian hair. It was thinning around the temples. His cheeks were sunken. His eyes were a light blue and seemed to have a penetrating gaze.

I began by asking him if the social worker had told him about what I was trying to do.

"No, she just told me that you wanted to meet me and that I should like to meet you."

Then I went into a long explanation. I said that I had been interested in congested city districts in my college study but had felt very remote from them. I hoped to study the problems in such a district. I felt I could do very little as an outsider. Only if I could get to know the people and learn their problems first hand would I be able to gain the understanding I needed.

Doc heard me out without any change of expression, so that I had no way of predicting his reaction. When I was finished, he asked: "Do you want to see the high life or the low life?"

"I want to see all that I can. I want to get as complete a picture of the community as possible."

"Well, any nights you want to see anything, I'll take you around. I can take you to the joints—gambling joints—I can take you around to the street corners. Just remember that you're my friend. That's all they need to know. I know these places, and, if I tell them that you're my friend, nobody will bother you. You just tell me what you want to see, and we'll arrange it."

The proposal was so perfect that I was at a loss for a moment as to how to respond to it. We talked a while longer, as I sought to get some pointers as to how I should behave in his company. He warned me that I might have to take the risk of getting arrested in a raid on a gambling joint but added that this was not serious. I only had to give a false name and then would get bailed out by the man that ran the place, paying only a five-dollar fine. I agreed to take this chance. I asked him whether I should gamble with others in the gambling joints. He said it was unnecessary and, for a greenhorn like myself, very inadvisable.

At last I was able to express my appreciation. "You know, the first steps of getting to know a community are the hardest. I could see things going with you that I wouldn't see for years otherwise."

"That's right. You tell me what you want to see, and we'll arrange it. When you want some information, I'll ask for it, and you listen. When you want to find out their philosophy of life, I'll start an argument and get it for you. If there's something else you want to get, I'll stage an act for you. Not a scrap, you know, but just tell me what you want, and I'll get it for you."

"That's swell. I couldn't ask for anything better. Now I'm going to try to fit in all right but, if at any time you see I'm getting off on the wrong foot, I want you to tell me about it."

"Now we're being too dramatic. You won't have any trouble. You come in as my friend. When you come in like that, at first everybody will treat you with respect. You can take a lot of liberties, and nobody will kick. After a while when they get to know you they will treat you like anybody else—you know, they say familiarity breeds contempt. But you'll never have any trouble. There's just one thing to watch out for. Don't spring [treat] people. Don't be too free with your money."

"You mean they'll think I'm a sucker?"

"Yes, and you don't want to buy your way in."

That was our beginning. At the time I found it hard to believe that I could move in as easily as Doc had said with his sponsorship. But that indeed was the way it turned out.

While I was taking my first steps with Doc, I was also finding a place to live in Cornerville. To meet people, to get to know them, to fit into their activities, required spending time with them—a lot of time day after day. Commuting to Cornerville, you might come in on a particular afternoon and evening only to discover that the people you intended to see did not happen to be around at the time. Or, even if you did see them, you might find the time passing entirely uneventfully. You might just be standing around with people whose only occupation was talking or walking about to try to keep themselves from being bored. Only if I lived in Cornerville would I ever be able to understand it and be accepted by it. Finding a place, however, was not easy. In such an overcrowded district a spare room was practically nonexistent. I might have been able to take a room in the Norton Street Settlement House, but I realized that I must do better than this if possible.

I got my best lead from the editor of a weekly English-language newspaper published for the Italian-American colony. I had talked to him before about my study and had found him sympathetic. Now I came to ask him for help in finding a room. He directed me to the Martinis, a family which operated a small restaurant. I went there for lunch and later consulted the son of the family. He was sympathetic but said that they had no place for any additional person. Still, I liked the place and enjoyed the food. I came back several times just to eat. On one occasion I met the editor, and he invited me to his table. We discussed my rooming problem again. I mentioned the possibility of living at the Norton Street House. He nodded but added: "It would be much better if you could be in a family. You would pick up the language much quicker, and you would get to know the people. But you want a nice family, an educated family. You don't want to get in with any low types. You want a real good family."

At this he turned to the son of the family with whom I had spoken and asked: "Can't you make some place for Mr. Whyte in the house here?"

Al Martini paused a moment and then said: "Maybe we can fix it up. I'll talk to Mama again."

So he did talk to Mama again, and they did find a place. In fact, he turned over to me his own room and moved in to share a double bed with the son of the cook. I protested mildly at this imposition, but everything had been decided—except for the money. They did not know what to charge me, and I did not know what to offer. Finally, after some fencing, I offered fifteen dollars a month, and they settled for twelve.

Physically, the place was livable, and it provided me with more than just a physical base. I had been with the Martinis for only a week when I discovered that I was much more than a roomer to them. I had been taking many of my meals in the restaurant and sometimes stopping in to chat with the family before I went to bed at night. Then one afternoon I was out at Harvard and found myself coming down with a bad cold. Since I still had my Harvard room, it seemed the sensible thing to do to stay overnight there. I did not think to tell the Martinis of my plan.

The next day when I was back in the restaurant for lunch, Al Martini greeted me warmly and then said that they had all been worried when I did not come home the night before. Mama had stayed up until two o'clock waiting for me. As I was just a young stranger in the city, she could visualize all sorts of things happening to me. Al told me that Mama had come to look upon me as one of the family. I was free to come and go as I pleased, but she wouldn't worry so much if she knew of my plans.

I was very touched by this plea and resolved thereafter to be as good a son as I could to the Martinis.

At first I communicated with Mama and Papa primarily in smiles and gestures. Papa knew no English at all, and Mama's knowledge was limited to one sentence which she would use when some of the young boys on the street were making noise below her window when she was trying to get her afternoon nap. She would then poke her head out of the window and shout: "Goddam-sonumabitcha! Getoutahere!"

Some weeks earlier, in anticipation of moving into the district, I had begun working on the Italian language myself with the aid of a Linguaphone. One morning now Papa Martini came by when I was talking to the phonograph record. He listened for a few moments in the hall trying to make sense out of this peculiar conversation. Then he burst in on me with fascinated exclamations. We sat down together while I demonstrated the machine and the method to him. After that he delighted in working with me, and I called him my language professor. In a short time we reached a stage where I could carry on simple conversations, and, thanks to the Linguaphone and Papa Martini, the Italian that came out apparently sounded authentic. He liked to try to pass me off to his friends as *paesano mio*—a man from his own home town in Italy.

Since my research developed so that I was concentrating almost exclusively upon the younger, English-speaking generation, my knowledge of Italian proved unnecessary for research purposes. Nevertheless, I feel certain that it was important in establishing my social position in Cornerville—even with that younger generation. There were schoolteachers and social workers who had worked in Cornerville for as much as twenty years and yet had made no effort to learn Italian. My effort to learn the language probably did more to establish the sincerity of my interest in the people than anything I could have told them of myself and my work.

My days with the Martinis would pass in this manner. I would get up in the morning around nine o'clock and go out to breakfast. Al Martini told me I could have breakfast in the restaurant, but, for all my desire to fit in, I never could take their breakfast of coffee with milk and a crust of bread.

After breakfast, I returned to my room and spent the rest of the morning, or most of it, typing up my notes regarding the previous day's events. I had lunch in the restaurant and then set out for the street corner. Usually I was back for dinner in the restaurant and then out again for the evening.

Usually I came home again between eleven and twelve o'clock, at a time when the restaurant was empty except perhaps for a few family friends. Then I might join Papa in the kitchen to talk as I helped him dry the dishes, or pull up a chair into a family conversation around one of the tables next to the kitchen. There I had a glass of wine to sip, and I could sit back and mostly listen but occasionally try out my growing Italian on them.

Though I made several useful contacts in the restaurant or through the family, it was not for this that the Martinis were important to me. There is a strain to doing such fieldwork. The strain is greatest when you are a stranger and are constantly wondering whether people are going to accept you. But, much as you enjoy your work, as long as you are observing and interviewing, you have a role to play, and you are not completely relaxed. It was a wonderful feeling at the end of a day's work to be able to come home to relax and enjoy myself with the family. Probably it would have been impossible for me to carry on such a concentrated study of Cornerville if I had not had such a home from which to go out and to which I might return.

*   *   *

I can still remember my first outing with Doc. We met one evening at the Norton Street House and set out from there to a gambling place a couple of blocks away. I followed Doc anxiously down the long, dark hallway at the back of a tenement building. I was not worried about the possibility of a police raid. I was thinking about how I would fit in and be accepted. The door opened into a small kitchen almost bare of furnishings and with the paint peeling off the walls. As soon as we went in the door, I took off my hat and began looking around for a place to hang it. There was no place. I looked around, and here I learned my first lesson in participant observation in Cornerville: Don't take off your hat in the house—at least not when you are among men. It may be permissible, but certainly not required, to take your hat off when women are around.

Doc introduced me as "my friend Bill" to Chichi, who ran the place, and to Chichi's friends and customers. I stayed there with Doc part of the time in the kitchen, where several men would sit around and talk, and part of the time in the other room watching the crap game.

There was talk about gambling, horse races, sex, and other matters. Mostly I just listened and tried to act friendly and interested. We had wine and coffee with anisette in it, with the fellows chipping in to pay for the refreshments. (Doc would not let me pay my share on this first occasion.) As Doc had predicted, no one asked me about myself, but he told me later that when I went to the men's room there was an excited burst of conversation in Italian and that he had to assure them that I was not a G-man. He said he told them flatly that I was a friend of his, and they agreed to let it go at that.

We went several more times together to Chichi's gambling joint, and then the time came when I dared to go in alone. When I was greeted in a natural and friendly manner, I felt that I was now beginning to find a place for myself in Cornerville.

When Doc did not go off to the gambling joint, he spent his time hanging around Norton Street, and I began hanging with him. At first, Norton Street meant only a place to wait until I could go somewhere else. Gradually, as I got to know the men better, I found myself becoming one of the Norton Street gang.

As I began to meet the men of Cornerville, I also met a few of the girls. One girl I took to a church dance. The next morning the fellows on the street corner were asking me: "How's your steady girl?" This brought me up short. I learned that going to the girl's house was something that you just did not do unless you hoped to marry her. Fortunately, the girl and her family knew that I did not know the local customs, so they did not assume that I was thus committed. However, this was a useful warning. After this time, even though I found some Cornerville girls exceedingly attractive, I never went out with them except on a group basis, and I did not make any more home visits either.

As I began hanging about Cornerville, I found that I needed an explanation for myself and for my study. As long as I was with Doc and vouched for by him, no one asked me who I was or what I was doing. When I circulated in other groups or even among the Nortons without him, it was obvious that they were curious about me.

I began with a rather elaborate explanation. I was studying the social history of Cornerville—but I had a new angle. Instead of working from the past up to the present, I was seeking to get a thorough knowledge of present conditions and then work from present to past. I was quite pleased with this explanation at the time, but nobody else seemed to care for it. It was apparently too involved to mean anything to Cornerville people.

I soon found that people were developing their own explanation about me: I was writing a book about Cornerville. This might seem entirely too vague an explanation, and yet it sufficed. I found that my acceptance in the district depended on the personal relationships I developed far more than upon any explanations I might give. Whether it was a good thing to write a book about Cornerville depended entirely on people's opinions of me personally. If I was all right, then my project was all right; if I was no good, then no amount of explanation could convince them that the book was a good idea.

Of course people did not satisfy their curiosity about me simply by questions that they addressed to me directly. They turned to Doc, for example, and asked him about me. Doc then answered the questions and provided any reassurance that was needed.

I learned early in my Cornerville period the crucial importance of having the support of the key individuals in any groups or organizations I was studying. Instead of trying to explain myself to everyone, I found I was providing far more information about myself and my study to leaders such as Doc than I volunteered to the average corner boy. I always tried to give the impression that I was willing and eager to tell just as much about my study as anyone wished to know, but it was only with group leaders that I made a particular effort to provide really full information.

While I worked more closely with Doc than with any other individual, I always sought out the leader in whatever group I was studying. I wanted not only sponsorship from him but also more active collaboration with the study. Since these leaders had the sort of position in the community that enabled them to observe much better than followers what was going on and since they were in general more skillful observers than the followers, I found that I had much to learn from a more active collaboration with them.

I learned to take part in the street corner discussions on baseball and sex. This required no special training, since the topics seemed to be matters of almost universal interest. I was not able to participate so actively in discussions of horse-racing. I did begin to follow the races in a rather general and amateur way. I am sure it would have paid me to devote more study to the *Morning Telegraph* and other racing sheets, but my knowledge of baseball at least ensured that I would not be left out of the street corner conversations.

While I avoided expressing opinions on sensitive topics, I found that arguing on some matters was simply part of the social pattern and that one could hardly participate without joining in the argument. I often found myself involved in heated but good-natured arguments about the relative merits of certain major-league ball players and managers. Whenever a girl or a group of girls would walk down the street, the fellows on the corner would make mental notes and later would discuss their evaluations of the females. These evaluations would run largely in terms of shape, and here I was glad to argue that Mary had a better "build" than

Anna, or vice versa. Of course, if any of the men on the corner happened to be personally attached to Mary or Anna, no searching comments would be made, and I, too, would avoid this topic.

Sometimes I wondered whether just hanging on the street corner was an active enough process to be dignified by the term "research." Perhaps I should be asking these men questions. However, one has to learn when to question and when not to question as well as what questions to ask.

I learned this lesson one night in the early months when I was with Doc in Chichi's gambling joint. A man from another part of the city was regaling us with a tale of the organization of gambling activity. I had been told that he had once been a very big gambling operator, and he talked knowingly about many interesting matters. He did most of the talking, but the others asked questions and threw in comments, so at length I began to feel that I must say something in order to be part of the group. I said: "I suppose the cops were all paid off?"

The gambler's jaw dropped. He glared at me. Then he denied vehemently that any policemen had been paid off and immediately switched the conversation to another subject. For the rest of that evening I felt very uncomfortable.

The next day Doc explained the lesson of the previous evening. "Go easy on that 'who,' 'what,' 'why,' 'when,' 'where' stuff, Bill. You ask those questions, and people will clam up on you. If people accept you, you can just hang around, and you'll learn the answers in the long run without even having to ask the questions."

I found that this was true. As I sat and listened, I learned the answers to questions that I would not even have had the sense to ask if I had been getting my information solely on an interviewing basis. I did not abandon questioning altogether, of course. I simply learned to judge the sensitiveness of the question and my relationship to the people so that I only asked a question in a sensitive area when I was sure that my relationship to the people involved was very solid.

*   *   *

At first I concentrated upon fitting into Cornerville, but a little later I had to face the question of how far I was to immerse myself in the life of the district. I bumped into that problem one evening as I was walking down the street with the Nortons [a group of young men from the neighborhood]. Trying to enter into the spirit of the small talk, I cut loose with a string of obscenities and profanity. The walk came to a momentary halt as they all stopped to look at me in surprise. Doc shook his head and said: "Bill, you're not supposed to talk like that. That doesn't sound like you."

I tried to explain that I was only using terms that were common on the street corner. Doc insisted, however, that I was different and that they wanted me to be that way.

This lesson went far beyond the use of obscenity and profanity. I learned that people did not expect me to be just like them; in fact, they were interested and pleased to find me different, just so long as I took a friendly interest in them. Therefore, I abandoned my efforts at complete immersion. My behavior was nevertheless affected by street corner life. When John Howard first came down from Harvard to join me in the Cornerville study, he noticed at once that I talked in Cornerville in a manner far different from that which I used at Harvard. This was not a matter of the use of profanity or obscenity, nor did I affect the use of ungrammatical expressions. I talked in the way that seemed natural to me, but what was natural in Cornerville was different from what was natural at Harvard. In Cornerville, I found myself putting much more animation into my speech, dropping terminal *g*'s, and using gestures much more actively.

As I became accepted by the Nortons and by several other groups, I tried to make myself pleasant enough so that people would be glad to have me around. And, at the same time, I tried to avoid influencing the group, because I wanted to study the situation as unaffected by my presence as possible. Thus, throughout my Cornerville stay, I avoided accepting office or leadership positions in any of the groups, with a single exception. At one time I was nominated as secretary of the Italian Community Club. My first impulse was to decline the nomination, but then I reflected that the secretary's job is normally considered simply a matter of dirty work—writing the minutes and handling the correspondence. I accepted and found that I could write a very full account of the progress of the meeting as it went on under the pretext of keeping notes for the minutes.

While I sought to avoid influencing individuals or groups, I tried to be helpful in the way a friend is expected to help in Cornerville. When one of the boys had to go downtown on an errand and wanted company, I went with him. When somebody was trying to get a job and had to write a letter about himself, I helped him to compose it, and so on. This sort of behavior presented no problem, but, when it came to the matter of handling money, it was not at all clear just how I should behave. Of course, I sought to spend money on my friends just as they did on me. But what about lending money? It is expected in such a district that a man will help out his friends whenever he can, and often the help needed is financial. I lent money on several occasions, but I always felt uneasy about it. Naturally, a man appreciates it at the time you lend him the money, but how does he feel later when the time has come to pay, and he is not able to do so? Perhaps he is embarrassed and tries to avoid your company. On such occasions I tried to reassure the individual and tell him that I knew he did not have it just then and that I was not worried about it. Or I even told him to forget about the debt altogether. But that did not wipe it off the books; the uneasiness remained. I learned that it is possible to do a favor for a friend and cause a strain in the relationship in the process.

I know no easy solution to this problem. I am sure there will be times when the researcher would be extremely ill advised to refuse to make a personal loan. On the other hand, I am convinced that, whatever his financial resources, he should not look for opportunities to lend money and should avoid doing so whenever he gracefully can.

If the researcher is trying to fit into more than one group, his fieldwork becomes more complicated. There may be times when the groups come into conflict with each other, and he will be expected to take a stand. There was a time in the spring of 1937 when the boys arranged a bowling match between the Nortons and the Italian Community Club. Doc bowled for the Nortons. Fortunately, my bowling at this time had not advanced to a point where I was in demand for either team, and I was able to sit on the sidelines. From there I tried to applaud impartially the good shots of both teams, although I am afraid it was evident that I was getting more enthusiasm into my cheers for the Nortons.

My first spring in Cornerville served to establish for me a firm position in the life of the district. I had only been there several weeks when Doc said to me: "You're just as much of a fixture around this street corner as that lamppost." Perhaps the greatest event signaling my acceptance on Norton Street was the baseball game that Mike Giovanni organized against the group of Norton Street boys in their late teens. It was the old men who had won glorious victories in the past against the rising youngsters. Mike assigned me to a regular position on the team, not a key position perhaps (I was stationed in right field), but at least I was there. When it was my turn to bat in the last half of the ninth inning, the score was tied, there were two outs, and the bases were loaded. As I reached down to pick up my bat, I heard some of the fellows suggesting to Mike that he ought to put in a pinch-hitter. Mike answered them in a loud voice that must have been meant for me: "No, I've got confidence in Bill Whyte. He'll come through in the clutch." So, with Mike's confidence to buck me up, I went up there, missed two swings, and then banged a hard grounder through the hole between second and short. At least that is where they told me it went. I was so busy getting down to first base that I did not know afterward whether I had reached there on an error or a base hit.

That night, when we went down for coffee, Danny presented me with a ring for being a regular fellow and a pretty good ball player. I was particularly impressed by the ring, for it had been made by hand. Danny had started with a clear amber die discarded from his crap game and over long hours had used his lighted cigarette to burn a hole through it and to round the corners so that it came out a heart shape on top. I assured the fellows that I would always treasure the ring.

Perhaps I should add that my game-winning base hit made the score 18–17, so it is evident that I was not the only one who had been hitting the ball. Still, it was a wonderful feeling to come through when they were counting on me, and it made me feel still more that I belonged on Norton Street.

Prostitution, Drug Use, and AIDS

CLAIRE STERK

Claire Sterk came to the United States from the Netherlands in 1986 as part of an exchange program between Erasmus University and the City University of New York's Center for Social Research. She had conducted research among prostitute and drug-using subcultures in the Netherlands for eight years. It was in the United States, however, that she became involved in AIDS research.

Sterk notes that in recent years there has been greater appreciation for ethnographic research as a means of providing background information for the evaluation of statistical data—that is, to find out about the people behind the facts. Populations "at risk" for AIDS—particularly prostitutes and intravenous drug users—constitute subcultures similar to those Sterk had studied in the past. They are best approached using the techniques of ethnographic research, especially observation and in-depth interviews. The use of these techniques allows the researcher to learn about sensitive issues that cannot be explored through more frequently used techniques such as questionnaires.

In the late 1980s Sterk conducted observational research in Newark, Jersey City, and New York City. The focus of her research was the behavior and attitudes of drug users and prostitutes, with emphasis on the impact of AIDS. Sterk was especially interested in discovering whether and to what extent women who become involved in prostitution through cocaine and crack use are at risk of contracting AIDS.

Although Sterk remains an outsider to the groups she is observing, her presence is accepted by members of those groups because she is "out there when they are out there"—in motels and hotels, brothels and escort services, shooting galleries and crack houses. She admits that she does not always feel safe in those environments (she is careful to ensure that a friend or colleague knows where she is); she also points out that safety depends largely on the attitude of the researcher: "These are human beings with feelings and emotions. If you care about them, they will care about you." During one two-month period she attended the funerals of seven women she knew from the street who had died of AIDS.

In this selection Sterk describes some of her experiences in the field and her feelings about them.

During the summer of 1986 I began conducting research among drug users and prostitutes in the New York metropolitan area. I had studied comparable groups in the Netherlands and was interested in discovering similarities and differences between the ways of life of these populations on both sides of the Atlantic Ocean. One can argue that turning tricks and shooting dope are the same all over the world. In reality, however, there are differences created by varying cultural circumstances. For example, in New York, where prostitution is illegal, the pimp plays a more important role in the prostitute's life than is the case in the Netherlands. When it comes to drugs, significant differences accrue from the fact that Dutch policies regarding drugs are more liberal than U.S. policies; moreover, crack has not yet become popular in the Netherlands.

Most of my research was done in Manhattan and Brooklyn and in northeastern New Jersey. Prostitutes and drug users frequently travel between New York and New Jersey. The two regions are close enough together so that the time it takes to travel between them amounts to less than thirty minutes. Operating in two adjacent states has advantages if one is involved in illegal activities; for one thing, it enables one to avoid an arrest warrant. If the police are seeking prostitutes in New York, the women simply shift their operation across the state line. Those living in New Jersey also cite economic reasons for commuting: In a large city like New York it is easier to make money, while the costs of living are significantly lower in New Jersey.

Before undertaking ethnographic research among people who are involved in deviant and very often illegal activities, one must locate the target population and determine how best to approach potential informants. With the help of colleagues, taxi drivers, and others, I was able to identify prostitute "strolls" and drug copping areas. I began visiting these neighborhoods and tried to get a sense of key events and characters by hanging out there. This gave me a chance to familiarize myself with the area while at the same time enabling the "regulars" to get to know my "face." Knowing where to go and recognizing faces, however, is only the beginning of a research effort. One can learn only so much through observation. The researcher must interact with the people he or she is studying.

A researcher—a stranger—cannot simply walk up to a potential informant and start chatting with him or her, especially if the informant is involved in illegal activities. When initiating a conversation, the researcher must justify his or her presence and indicate the desire for interaction, usually without knowing whether the other person can be trusted. Gaining trust is very important.

My acceptance into the prostitute subculture came about in a rather unexpected way. I had been walking around on the stroll for days and nobody wanted to talk to me. I recognized a few of the prostitutes from earlier visits, but they ignored me. But finally one of them, Ann, responded to my greeting. In a very cynical tone she asked me if I was looking for something special. For a second I did not know what to say. I answered very vaguely that I was just walking around. She thought this to be a silly answer and asked aggressively where I was from. I told her Amsterdam and started talking more openly. She teased me because I was getting red in the face. I kept on talking, glad that I had finally caught somebody's attention. I told her I was interested in prostitution and wanted to find out about the situation in the United States.

Ann challenged my knowledge, and apparently I answered her questions appropriately. She started talking about one of her girlfriends who was in "the life" and had moved to Europe with a boyfriend, an American GI stationed in West Germany. After the relationship ended, she began working in the sex business in Amsterdam. I was familiar with the club Ann mentioned and knew its owner. Ann began to open up and talk more to me, but she was careful. Another prostitute came by to check out what we were doing. Ann became very defensive about her relationship with me. She told the other woman to knock off, and described me as one of her friends.

I was fortunate, not only because Ann was willing to talk with me but also because I was not completely naive. Being somewhat familiar with the life style of the persons studied is of great value to a researcher in the field. The researcher will never have the knowledge of an insider without becoming a member of the group being studied, but a good ethnographer will try to find out about the norms and values of the world he or she is studying—always keeping in mind that too much knowledge might be seen as threatening.

In another situation I gained the confidence of an informant named Mo by demonstrating my knowledge of three-card monte, a popular con game. A white woman from Europe is not supposed to have such knowledge. My "showing off" made Goldman, a pimp, curious. Goldman, who has a penchant for big cars and lots of jewelry, said to me, "Damn, baby, you know what you are talking about. That's good, though; otherwise they would try to fool you. You have to prove yourself; showing off is what matters. Don't show off too much, now. We don't need wiseguys around here. I will tell you what to do and I will give my ladies instructions. If you are nice we won't have any problems."

While talking with potential informants, the researcher also develops a sense of who the important "players" are. It is necessary to gain their trust. They provide an entree into the community under study by facilitating the process of gaining the trust of others. Ideally, key contacts are individuals who are known and respected by other members of the community. Ann, for example, was one of the "main ladies"; Mo, a three-card monte player, was viewed as a good hustler; and Goldman was a well-known pimp.

During the initial stages of my research I was not the only one exploring and wondering. Respondents often tried to place me in impossible positions. Rumors spread that I was a potential prostitute, a drug user, or an undercover police officer. I was friendly, and so were my respondents, but simultaneously they were contemplating the possibility that I had a "hidden agenda." Mistrust and suspicion were ever-present, even in contacts with key respondents. Ann, for example, would, when I least expected it, ask me to repeat a certain story I had told her. She also explained to me that in trusting me she was taking chances herself. She would be blamed if it turned out that I could not be trusted, and this would have negative repercussions for her reputation.

One of the main lessons I have learned is that I must be honest and open about my intentions and that I must be constantly alert to the feelings of respondents. Being trusted does not assure acceptance. Again and again people challenged my presence and tested my intentions to "see if I was for real." Street life seems to require that one never develop permanent trust for anyone. One must continually check and reassess.

On one occasion I was standing on the street where the prostitutes were usually picked up by their customers. It was a nice evening, but business was slow. Pat, one of the streetwalkers, started telling me how they had been observing me. "We did not know if you were for real," she said. "It looked like we could trust you, but that could be your game. We decided to leave you alone and see how you would handle the tricks. I never forget the time the guy kept waving at you and you just looked around to see what we were doing. You couldn't have done better. He is still one of my regulars."

Pat and I now can laugh together about that situation. I referred the customer to her, telling him I was just hanging out on my night off.

There were many other episodes in which people tested my integrity, either by observing my reactions or by asking me for favors. The prostitutes would ask me to hold their purses, or they would share stories and check later to see if I had gossiped. They expected me to buy them a cup of coffee or a sandwich and to drive them around as if I were a cab driver.

Ann advised me: "You have to be nice, but don't act like a softie!" I was also (unknowingly) used as "bait" for customers. Our tacit agreement was that I would not alienate the men who stopped to talk to me; instead, I would direct them to the "working girls."

Setting limits was a major issue. Repeatedly I had to convince drug users that I had no interest in buying stolen goods, and I often had to demonstrate to pimps that I was not interested in working for them. I was involved in the groups I was studying, but I remained an outsider in many ways. I was an outsider not only because I was not an active participant or because of my Dutch accent, but also because frequently I was one of the few, if not the only, white person in the area. This made me highly visible and easy to recognize. I was teasingly referred to as "the white girl," "Whitie," or "Miss Whitie," and one of the pimps told me he had a special deal for white ladies. The teasing had a bonding effect; several women expressed this by saying, "You are my only white friend" or "You are a nice white person."

During the many hours I spent with the prostitutes, of whom many were drug users, their pimps, drug partners, and dealers seldom interrupted their illegal activities because of my presence. Occasionally I was asked to leave the area because my presence was seen as a problem. The drug-using activities were generally covert and usually took place indoors, whereas the prostitution deals were more public.

Most of the women would talk with me about their work if I asked them about it, although they seldom discussed their work among themselves. (An exception was talk about tricks who could not be trusted or were too demanding.) Frequently they told me stories, mainly dealing with their emotions, that they did not share with one another. In short, I was treated as a trusted outsider who had a sense of what was going on in their lives.

My outsider status was validated on the occasions when I was seen as incompetent on the street. For example, everybody enjoyed my initial inability to anticipate police presence. I would be stopped and told to leave; my hidden audience would later make fun of me, but at the same time ensure that I didn't get into trouble. They also informed me about the dangers involved in being out on the street. "Prostitutes are not staying out late anymore," I was told. "A group of four young men have been coming into the area. They wait until it gets dark and start assaulting the women. The moment one of the women is alone, they jump on her, take her money, and hurt her."

The women became even more frightened after one of them was killed. Paula said to me, "You should not come here after dark. We are from the street . . . I am not saying that I am stronger than you are, but you do not have to be out here. I won't come unless I have to. I am even storing dope so I don't have to go out late at night."

It was during these moments that I realized that I would always be an outsider. No matter how much time I spent with them, I could always return to another world, a world of safety and stability. I often felt bad about this, and about the fact that there was nothing I could do to change their situation. These feelings became stronger the more I was confronted with the consequences of the AIDS epidemic.

By now it is widely known that many groups besides homosexual males are at risk of contracting AIDS. Among those groups are intravenous drug users, sexually active individuals and their sexual partners, and their babies. In the New York metropolitan area infection rates among intravenous drug users are as high as they are among homosexual men. During the hours I spent talking with respondents, I tried to sensitize them to the risks they were taking, and we talked about the possibility of modifying their behavior. Condom use and needle sharing were frequent topics of discussion.

One evening I was sitting with three of the prostitutes. An outreach worker had visited the stroll and they had plenty of condoms. We were joking, but at the same time we were talking about safe sex. The women's opinions about condom use varied. Laura said she never used them. Cindy would not have sex without a condom, and Maria used condoms with her tricks but not with her boyfriend. Maria's boyfriend gets upset if she so much as shows him a condom. All three agreed that it is easier to propose the use of condoms with tricks than with steadies. But as Laura pointed out, "I'm not going to fight about it. What's the big deal? He'll turn around and find somebody else, if that's what he wants. I always check to see if they are clean anyhow."

Our conversation shifted to blow jobs. Their mood was playful but serious. Cindy told me to taste a rubber before I made any further comments. She has learned how to use a condom while having oral sex without the customer knowing it. She is very proud of this skill and provided a demonstration. Giggling, we tried to follow her instructions. I do not know if this made a lasting impression on Laura and Maria, but at least we brought the issue out into the open.

On another occasion one of the prostitutes, Angie, said that she didn't think using condoms made any difference. "I'm already in the gutter," she said. "I feel sick, am losing weight. I'm going to die anyhow. What fucking difference does it make?"

We talked about knowledge, attitudes, and behavior, and about the relevance of testing for HIV antibodies. Sometimes I initiated these discussions; at other times I was drawn into an ongoing conversation. The respondents could be divided into two groups. One stressed the importance of testing because it reveals the individual's current condition. Those who test negative are often motivated to change their behavior to avoid seroconverting; those who test positive can take steps to avoid spreading the virus. Another group opposed testing because there is no cure for AIDS. Their main question was, "What is the sense of getting tested if there is nothing you can do about it? It only fucks you up."

As a researcher, I had difficulty taking a stand on this issue. Generally I encouraged testing because of the respondents' involvement in risky behaviors.

Respondents who had tested positive for HIV antibodies wanted to discuss their status with me. Because we had already developed a relationship, they trusted me more than they would a "strange" counselor. Jacky, a 24-year-old street prostitute, confided in me: "I can't talk with them folks. They are straight or faggots and don't know what the hell they are talking about. I don't need a preacher telling me what to do. They better get their own act together. I'm scared and don't want to die. What am I going to tell my old man?"

AIDS changed the relationship between me and my respondents. I began to be seen as a sort of on-the-stroll counselor, even though I did not have a lot to offer besides listening and trying to make appropriate referrals. I remember one case in particular: that of Micky and Jeanne.

Micky was 32 years old; his girlfriend Jeanne was 26. They both injected drugs and smoked crack. Micky went out and "did his thing" to get cash, and Jeanne turned tricks when he did not have enough money to support both of them. Then Micky started feeling sick. He was so tired he could not work. Jeanne started working more hours while a friend of Micky's watched her back in exchange for some dope. Jeanne, Micky, and I spent a lot of time together. One day he started asking questions about AIDS. He was going to see a doctor because he felt very sick.

Three days later Jeanne told me he was in the hospital. He got very sick and an ambulance had to pick him up. She did not know what to do. A week later Micky was out on the street again. He refused to sign a form and the hospital let him go as soon as he could walk. While in the hospital Micky was tested for AIDS; he tested positive. He did not want to talk with a counselor.

I tried to persuade Micky and Jeanne to seek help, but they felt that no one understood them. They also wanted to continue to get high, each with their own syringe. Micky said, "I'm going to die and I want to enjoy things. I can make that decision myself." In a few months Micky died. Jeanne was never tested and went on working.

One of the ethical questions one faces as a researcher is what to do when an infected drug user continues to share hypodermic sets or an infected prostitute continues to have sex with her customers and/or boyfriend without using prophylactics. I frequently dealt with individuals who were seropositive but did not protect others against infection. One of them said to me, "They know as well as I do what the deal is. In this life everybody takes care of himself. If you want to take chances, it's your responsibility. I don't have to warn others."

My conversations with respondents about changing drug-using and sexual behaviors became more concrete as more people became sick and died of AIDS. The people who share a stroll or a copping area form a relatively closed community. Because of the visible effects of AIDS on members of the community, issues like drugs and sex came to be discussed more openly. Almost everybody I spoke with knew the ways in which the AIDS virus can be spread, and conversations about the use of condoms and the sharing of "works" became more common. Increasingly, I was not the person who brought up these issues. Respondents came up to me and asked me questions, or simply wanted to talk about what was going on. The threat posed by AIDS to almost everybody in the community made people more open. It also made them feel more vulnerable. It is scary to see your buddies get sick and die.

The increasing number of friends and acquaintances dying of AIDS affected me deeply. Attending funerals became a way of showing my concern and respect. In one brief period six people from one research site died. I had known four of them fairly well and had interviewed the other two. The latter were street prostitutes who used drugs intravenously; the others included a drug-using prostitute, a male hustler, and two intravenous drug users, one female and the other male. All had lived in close proximity and had frequent dealings with one another. The social linkages among them had been strong. Many of their friends had known all or some of them.

I was upset by the high rate of death among the people I was studying. I mentioned this to one of the women, who answered, "We all have this problem. It is going to get worse. Over half of the people around here are infected. Can you imagine . . . If you are out on the street long enough you learn to cope with everything. Getting sad or scared is not going to help. We have to survive. You have to set limits."

After this conversation I decided that things were getting out of hand. I discussed my feelings with several people, including colleagues and "field friends." In one neighborhood the situation had become so bad that children were referring to funeral cars as "AIDS wagons." But then something happened that made me realize that alongside of death there is always life.

A Hispanic woman, clearly ill, was trying to walk toward a nearby hospital. She was visibly pregnant. I approached her, and while we were talking her water broke. I realized that I didn't have time to get a car, so I jumped into the middle of the street and stopped the first car that came along. It was occupied by a middle-aged white couple. While I was explaining what was happening the woman groaned and said the baby, her second child, was coming. Although we were less than five minutes from the hospital, the baby was born in the back seat of the car. The woman in the front seat started crying and saying how thankful she was that we had chosen their car. The man walked away, sickened by the mess in the car. The mother, Carmen, cried and looked happily at her baby as she carried it into the hospital. I stood around, confused and disoriented. My clothes and hands were dirty. I was overwhelmed by having been involved in the birth of a baby on the same streets where people were dying of AIDS.

The AIDS epidemic has given ethnographic research a new dimension. AIDS has made me more aware of the fact that every researcher is affected by the work he or she does. One cannot remain neutral and uninvolved; even as an outsider, the researcher is part of the community under study and must recognize that fact.

On Studying
South Chicago

WILLIAM KORNBLUM

*In the 1960s and 1970s a number of sociological studies focused on social stratifi-
cation and politics in particular communities. Among them was* Blue Collar
Community, *William Kornblum's study of the steelworkers of South Chicago.
Kornblum spent more than three years observing working-class politics—the politics
of the trade union and the local ward—in a community that had been dominated
by heavy manufacturing for more than a century. He was attracted to South Chicago not only by its dramatic labor struggles but also by its intricate ethnic and
communal life.*

*Although it lost much of its employment base in the late 1970s and the 1980s,
South Chicago remains a large steel mill community within the city limits of metropolitan Chicago. Its population includes members of almost every major ethnic and
racial group that has settled in American industrial communities over the last
century—Northern Europeans, Eastern Europeans, Mexicans, and blacks. Although the European immigrants are often lumped together as "white ethnics," they
are extremely diverse in cultural terms; the differing cultural backgrounds of the
more recent black and Mexican immigrants have also contributed to the cultural
complexity of this working-class community.*

*Despite the cultural antagonisms of the different racial and ethnic groups that
have settled in South Chicago, Kornblum found abundant evidence of worker solidarity as reflected in trade union activity and political loyalties. His observations*

impressed him with the strength and variety of the interpersonal networks formed by the leaders of different socioeconomic groups in an effort to aggregate their political power. Instead of a large number of alienated blue-collar workers, he found an intricate set of interconnected groups and coalitions that produced an unexpected degree of social cohesion.

During the time in which Kornblum was conducting his research, he and his wife lived in South Chicago and made many friends among their neighbors. He also participated actively in local political campaigns and was employed for six months as a subforeman in one of the area's steel mills. The steelworkers union president who found him the job told him it would allow him to "get a real education inside the mill." As the following selection shows, it certainly did.

In the initial stage of a community study the researcher frequently hesitates to make commitments. The choice of a specific set of research sites and questions, the selection of a place to live, a group of people to become friendly with, and a way of explaining one's purposes to residents, all seem like irreversible decisions. During this rather normal period of "hanging back" and surveying the diversity of people and situations, one is likely to feel extremely alien and isolated. Perhaps for this reason many fieldwork projects begin with the author seeking out a place to become known, one which advances familiarity with the people but does not necessitate lasting commitment. Thus in *Street Corner Society* William F. Whyte explains how he became friendly with the family of an Italian restauranteur who provided him with a congenial base from which to plan his further participation in the community's life. Following this precedent I found a Serbian immigrant restaurant run by an enormous peasant woman and her very slight husband. Radmilla and Mike appreciated my halting attempts to converse with them in Serbo-Croatian, and they introduced me to the establishment's regulars. The majority of the patrons were Serbian immigrant men in their mid-thirties to early forties. Almost all were steelworkers. On Friday and Saturday nights they filled the restaurant to eat, drink, and dance to the popular music of contemporary Serbia.

One Friday night I entered in the middle of a brawl, which I learned was the continuation of an argument started in the steel mill three blocks away. While the electric guitar and accordion ensemble played on, three or four men were shouting in Serbo-Croatian and pushing each other. At this point Radmilla, who weighed at least 250 pounds, stepped into the crowd to separate the antagonists. As she did this, a man named Stanko seized a bar stool but she pushed him away easily. Infuriated, he threw the stool at her husband, Mike, who had had just enough to drink that he did not duck in time and was struck on the head and shoulders. In the ensuing melee I tended to the fallen Mike while Radmilla cleared the tavern and restored calm. After that evening I became a welcome friend in their tavern and I felt I had found a place where I did belong in the community. It soon became apparent, however, that I was viewing the ethnic group and the community from one of its most peripheral social circles.

Although it was a congenial spot to stop on my visits to South Chicago, most of the patrons at the Neretva Lounge were among the most recent arrivals to the city from Serbia. As such they were generally men without families, or whose families had remained in Yugoslavia. Along with an assortment of non-Serbian alcoholics and a few transient Mexicans the group was quite distant from the more established networks of South Chicago Serbian ethnicity. Socially they were even farther from the networks of people who involved themselves in the life of the larger community. The people at the Neretva were somewhat involved with other Serbian groups in establishing a new Serbian church. Since they had broken away from the church established by the pioneer generation of Serbian settlers, there was a great deal of tension in the relationships between these factions. The native-born Serbians and Croatians referred to the immigrants as DP's while their own ethnic identity and social institutions seemed to me to be largely the product of their experience in South Chicago and other industrial communities of this society. To learn more about the differences between native-born and immigrant South Slavs, I began spending more time among native-born Serbian and Croatian residents. Thus at the end of 1967 I began looking for a place to settle in the community.

As I began hunting for an apartment, it became clear why I had chosen to study this community rather than other South Slavic neighborhoods elsewhere in the metropolitan area. South Chicago fascinated me. I had never seen such heavy industry at close range, and I was awed by the immensity of the steel mills and the complexity of the water and rail arteries which crisscrossed the area's neighborhoods. I saw more of the spectrum of cultural groups which had settled and built the community. Thus, I was beginning to see that my study would have to concern itself as much with the larger community as it would with the cultural and social adaptations of Serbian and Croatian settlers. In the impressive series of community studies compiled by Chicago sociologists there were none which explicitly focused on this type of community. Therefore, I came to feel that in addition to studying the cultural and social adaptations of South Slavic people, my work should also include material on this important industrial community.

This was also the period of increasingly bitter sentiment against the war in Indochina. Campus political groups were continually debating the issue of how to involve "the working class" in antiwar activities, or if such a task could be accomplished at all. Surprisingly few of my university friends had any knowledge even of the working-class communities nearest to the University of Chicago. Mention of the fact that I was spending time in the steel mill neighborhoods of South Chicago often brought the response, "Oh, you mean all those neighborhoods around Gary?" Chicago's mill neighborhoods begin on 79th Street, just nineteen blocks from the university, but they are often perceived as being closer to Gary, more than thirty miles to the south. Indeed, the blue collar neighborhoods which begin in South Chicago bear great similarity to those continuing past Gary to South Bend, Indiana. I thus resolved that whatever else it accomplished, my study should attempt to show what life is like in such places. It should show what political questions actually do challenge the residents, and among these would likely be the issue of working-class race relations.

In March 1968 my wife and I moved into a tenement flat in Irondale, one of the oldest neighborhoods of first settlement in the community. Irondale was a logical choice for a number of reasons. First, it had been one of the most popular neighborhoods for South Slavic immigrant settlement earlier in the century. It still retained a significant population of older settlers plus an increasing number of younger "DP" families. Second, it had been the site of the severe racial rioting which I read about in Frank London Brown's novel *Trumbull Park*. The late black author had vividly described the awful experience of trying to survive (with his family) in the neighborhood's housing project. Fourteen years had passed since these riots, but they were well remembered in Chicago. I suspected, rightly as it turned out, that we would be living among many of the people who had done the rioting. We would have a chance to see the issues from their perspective and learn how the intervening years had softened their violently defensive behavior. What I did not fully understand, however, was that Irondale was also becoming a Mexican neighborhood. In various ways the Mexicans were acting as a transition group to the eventual settlement of more black families in the neighborhood.

Irondale's older white families continued to be extremely sensitive to racial issues and bitterly opposed to racial integration of their neighborhood. Since I was then meeting many of the leaders of the violent resistance that had occurred in the Trumbull Park riots, I was also coming in for a good deal of scrutiny and suspicion. Although I wanted to get to know the central figures in the South Deering Improvement Association, this was not a simple matter for an outsider. If I was to hear how these men and women felt about the Trumbull Park riots, I would need greater access to their private haunts, especially the basement of the American Legion Hall, where the association had a bar that was off limits to the public.

Fortunately, as an ethnographer I am blessed with a unique asset: a wife with a quick wit, a ready laugh, a genuine interest in other people, and a willingness to come with me on almost any adventure. One day I informed her that I had volunteered the two of us to work for the Improvement Association at its food stands at the July 4 Trumbull Park Festival. We worked all day cooking and serving grinder sandwiches, and all the key members of the Association worked with us. It soon became clear that Susan was a master of mental arithmetic and could make change in an instant with no mistakes. I, on the other hand, had a strong back and was good for hauling boxes of food and soft drinks. All day Susan cracked jokes with the neighbors and with the leaders of the Improvement Association. At the end of the day we were invited to the private bar, where Susan was given the honor of assisting in counting the money and was then invited to take a hand in the poker game. I served as a friendly and clearly nonthreatening onlooker.

After that occasion we were accepted everywhere in the neighborhood. When Susan was expecting our first child, our popularity with many of the women in the neighborhood increased even further, and we were increasingly invited to major social affairs like weddings and large union gatherings. That Thanksgiving we received not one but two free turkeys, one from the ward political organization, via the neighborhood precinct captain, and one from the local church (since our part of the neighborhood was quite the poorest section).

When our first child was born, after a year in Irondale, we began spending a great deal of time with our Mexican neighbors because they were more likely to have young children than our somewhat older South Slavic and Italian neighbors. From them, and especially from the Mexican youth groups which hung out on our corner, I learned that there was continual conflict with the Mexicans from the Millgate and Bessemer Park neighborhoods on the other side of the community. Similar to the opposition which existed between native-born and immigrant South Slavic groups, this opposition between the Mexican neighborhoods conformed quite closely to the pattern of "ordered segmentation" which Gerald Suttles analyzed in *The Social Order of the Slum*. The first level of opposition or conflict between ethnic groups in the community did not involve different cultural groups but occurred among equivalent territorial groups of the same ethnicity.

The next level of opposition tended to unify diverse groups from Irondale against those in geographically separated neighborhoods such as the East Side. On the other hand, all the residents whom I spoke to referred to the entire area as South Chicago, and they considered themselves residents of that community.

This perception seemed somewhat paradoxical. On the one hand so many people I met were generally involved in provincial feuding within their ethnic groups, and on the other they were in various ways quite clearly becoming involved in the life of the larger community. To investigate this problem it again seemed important to become familiar with the

way the larger industrial and political institutions of the community operated. In particular it would be necessary to understand how experiences
in the steel mills, the labor unions, and the political institutions of the
community in various ways modified the residents' notions of which
groups and individuals are worthy of their trust. In answering these questions I believed I would also begin to understand the processes whereby
so many cultural groups had learned not only to coexist with each other
but to adjust their basic patterns of ethnic social organization to compete
in the class and status systems of the community and the larger society.
From the start of my work I had been meeting and interviewing people
whom I identified as leaders of various cultural and political institutions
in the community. It appeared that I would need to follow their activities
at a much closer range.

Soon after moving into the community I had begun a systematic effort
to attend any and all public meetings in the community, to identify local
leaders, and to arrange to meet with them for an introduction or a formal
interview. Before long I learned to resist the "compulsion to confess"
which often troubles field researchers. Most people I met in the course
of my daily life were interested in why I had settled in the community. In
answering this question I explained that I was teaching at the nearby University of Indiana, Hammond extension, while my wife was a student at
the University of Illinois Circle Campus in the central city. The Irondale
location was a halfway point for both of us. This was true, and although
it omitted my main motives for settling in South Chicago, it made routine
social intercourse much easier. If to every tavern clique and candy store
acquaintance I had divulged my intentions to study the community, I
would have probably elicited some parody of life in sociological jargon.
But when I introduced myself to specific residents of the community, or
whenever I interviewed someone, I attempted to explain the goals of my
study as simply and consistently as I could, and the interview would generally proceed without misunderstanding of my goals.

Gradually, through these introductions and interviews I began to become friendly with a rather large number of political activists and neighborhood leaders. After introducing myself to a local labor leader, for example, I would then find myself meeting that person during my regular
round of visits to public places and community events. These encounters
would lead to new introductions and greater familiarity. By the end of my
first year in South Chicago I counted well over fifty persons who had
expressed interest in my study and were in various ways providing me
with information about the underlying meaning of the political and social
events I observed. Among the circles in which I was becoming more or
less accepted were a group of Italian and Serbian steelworkers from Irondale who ran the local union at one of the area's large mills, a group of

younger political activists from the East Side who met regularly to discuss community events and to plan political activities, two groups of ward political activists of mixed ethnicity, and friendship groups which met regularly in about fifteen taverns where I made rounds.

In addition to participating in the informal life of these groups I attended as many functions of the Serbian and Croatian ethnic groups as possible. Also, through the normal course of life among my Mexican neighbors I had many opportunities to observe the culture and social organization of Mexican neighborhood ethnic groups. Fieldwork was becoming more than a full-time occupation, and I often found myself dictating slurred field notes at 4:00 A.M. after a full day of meetings and social drinking in the area's taverns and political clubs. Despite the full schedule I had developed, I began to feel that the more I learned about the community through my friends and informants, the more necessary it was for me to commit myself to a greater degree to South Chicago's life style. I felt like a knowledgeable outsider who was missing some of the most important experiences of life in the community. At this time, in the middle of my second year of fieldwork in South Chicago, a friend whose opinion I highly valued, the Serbian president of a local steel union, confronted me with a serious challenge. "How can you really understand what goes on here," he asked, "if you've never spent any time inside a steel mill?" I replied that it had been my desire to work in a mill, that I agreed it was necessary, but when I had applied to work in one of the area's large mills a few months earlier I had been turned down because I had "too much education to push a broom in a laborer's job." Amused, my unionist friend asked me if I would like a job in the mill he represented. He assured me that he would arrange things so that my job would allow me to "get a real education inside the mill." Before I was given the job my friend called me one night to ask, "Bill, you're not one of these SDS guys, are you? You know there's a lot of talk these days about radicals coming into the mills to stir up trouble." I assured him that such was not my intention and within another week I was hired as a subforeman.

I approached my job in the mill with some embarassment. As a subforeman I was nonetheless a representative of management when most of my sympathies and many of my friendships were with rank-and-file workers. Outside the mills, in social circles frequented by steelworkers and their families, one rarely met any foremen or managerial officials, and indeed management was often spoken of with some disdain. Also, as a foreman I was not allowed to perform manual work since the union viewed that as an encroachment on workers' jobs in the plant. My job was to oversee and coordinate the work of about thirty men who were chippers, laborers, machine operators, cranemen, and loaders. As the men taught me how to accomplish my work with a minimum of conflict and disruption of their normal institutional arrangements with each other and with management, I began to see that my friend had situated me in a difficult job but one which was about the best position a sociologist could have had.

In performing my duties as subforeman I had to understand how the work on my end of the mill fit into the overall division of labor in the entire plant. As a managerial employee I could circulate relatively freely throughout the mill to learn how steel was produced and to converse informally with workers in hundreds of different occupations. Since mine was the lowest status managerial position possible, I represented little threat to anyone. Most of my rank-and-file peers were making more money than I was, and, as they delighted in pointing out, their jobs did not include the headache of being responsible to higher level managerial officials. In reflecting on the differences between my low level managerial position and the more narrowly circumscribed activities of the rank-and-file workers with whom I spent the bulk of my time, I began to understand from a personal viewpoint more of the meaning of unionism and labor bargaining for the average steelworker.

The other foremen with whom I worked were much more concerned about pleasing their superiors than were the rank-and-file workers. The latter were guaranteed advancement through the seniority system as long as they learned their jobs and performed them reliably. In case of trouble the workers could turn to their grievancemen and the union officials they had elected to intercede on their behalf in their dealings with management. The foremen had none of this protection. Although they claimed they did not need it, and indeed the vast majority of their superiors were considerate, experienced men, their occupational culture was full of stories of ambitious young foremen who had crossed high level officials at the wrong time and had been set back in their careers. None of our superiors in the rolling mill were vindictive types, but I was warned that Mr. W   , a high level manager who circulated throughout the entire plant, should be carefully avoided when he came into our mill.

Shortly thereafter, during a week when my turn was working nights, my general foreman warned me that the feared W   had been seen leaving the adjacent mill heading in the direction of my work area. I was advised to make sure my men were all working properly and then to go off on an errand elsewhere in the mill. Here I should note that company officials were not aware of my intention to write about mill work. I rationalized this situation by attempting to do my job so that my personal motives for being in the mill would not compromise the performance of my work. On this occasion, however, I did not heed the older foreman's well-intentioned advice. Instead I loitered in my work area to see for myself what an encounter with W   would be like. When he entered my area of the mill, he walked directly up to me. Without introducing himself, he barked a question which produced the following dialogue:

W: What's that steel being loaded into those cars?

Kornblum: Oh, that's a mixed order of spring steel and thirty foot rounds that we're trying to load before the switch comes in.

W: I can see what it is. Who is it for? Where's it going?

Kornblum: Well, let's see, I think it's for . . .

W: God dammit. Do you know who that steel is for or don't you?

Kornblum: I'm not sure.

W: You damn well better get off your dead cock and find out what's being done around here or you're not going to last. This is a steel mill and not a nursery school. We've got too many jagg offs like you who sit around with their thumbs up their assholes and don't know what's going on.

The official strode away leaving me trembling with anger and humiliation. I had worked in many blue collar jobs before entering the steel mill, and as a laborer on an East River construction dock in Manhattan I had seen corruption and violence which made the normal routine of mill work seem tame. Since I was doing a relatively good job as a new foreman in a mill beset with serious racial and ethnic cleavages, I did not believe I should be treated in this way by someone who had never seen me before. It is true that I should have known the answer to his question and he was justified in "chewing me out." But except in jest the foremen on the shop floor rarely spoke to their own men in such terms. The dictates of common sense and the watchful influence of union representatives usually prevented such confrontations between foremen and workers. In general such personal experiences as this made me a good deal more sensitive to the style and content of interactions in the mill and deepened my desire to understand the meaning of unionism in the context of my study. Thus I pursued this goal while I worked in the mill and later when I assisted my unionist friends in their political campaigns.

Many sociologists have regarded "informal organization" as an inevitable characteristic of industrial bureaucracies, but one which in the interest of rationality and productivity must be manipulated through the techniques of "industrial relations." Given the orientation of my research I could not view the issue in this way. The study of informal relations among the workers became another aspect of my inquiry into how steel production creates an occupational community inside the mill. I thus attempted to discover the conditions under which revelations of character on the job could be as important as ethnic and racial categories in guiding the workers' behavior. My run-in with W   , for example, immediately became the subject of gossip and bantering in work groups throughout the mill. "How could a kid with your education act like such a dummy?" asked the chief loader. This question launched a long philosophical discussion in the loaders' shanty. Most of the loaders worried that the incident would hurt my chances for advancement in the company. Others suggested that it should make me question the desirability of holding a job with management. Finally, a young Mexican loader, who was also a friend from the neighborhood, settled the argument in a statement which has remained in the front of my mind ever since. "What you guys don't understand," he stated, "is that Kornblum isn't stuck here like most of us stiffs. In his life he can do just about anything he really wants to do." Although perhaps somewhat obvious, this insight made me much more sensitive to the workers' attempts to express their own individuality throughout their careers in the steel mill. I also understood another side of this remark from my own difficulties in attempting to carry on my other fieldwork while remaining in the mill.

One morning after I had been working in the mill for almost six months I boarded a bus with a large group of Tenth Ward Spanish Speaking Democrats to attend the Chicago Democratic Day at the Illinois State Fair in Springfield. Since I had worked the previous night turn I immediately fell asleep. When I awoke about an hour later everyone on the bus was laughing at me. One of my neighbors had told those who did not know me that I was a worker at the Ford assembly plant down the road from our steel mill. He explained that I had fallen asleep and missed my stop. Some of South Chicago's Mexican activists still jokingly refer to me as "the guy from the Ford plant." This Springfield outing ended back in South Chicago about fifteen minutes before my shift began again in the mill. After eight hours of seeking places to steal a few minutes' sleep, I realized that I was reaching a point of diminishing returns in my participation inside the mill. Political events were rapidly accelerating in the outside community, and I could not become as involved in them as I wished because of the severe physical and temporal demands of mill work.

From the beginning of the research I had followed political campaigns and the careers of local politicians quite closely. At first I had attended meetings of campaign workers on both sides of the factional disputes in the community, thereby developing a large number of informants who supplied me with details of events I had witnessed. Generally it was necessary to compare carefully the accounts of a number of informants in order to compensate for individual biases and personal perceptions. At the same time I was beginning to feel that I had accumulated personal debts to many local groups, especially to my unionist friends and to many of my Slavic and Mexican neighbors. Working in the mill had brought me much more general acceptance in the community, but acceptance also subjected me to the same pressures to commit myself in partisan campaigns that others felt.

The pressure to become committed to other people is a general characteristic of community life in South Chicago, but during the time I lived in the community this pressure was probably as great as it had ever been. This was a time when the community was involved in sorting out the leadership of its most central institutions. For this reason all my friends and informants found themselves in one way or another drawn into competition between aggregations of community groups. It seemed that only the most financially secure or socially marginal people could afford not to take sides. This same spirit of partisanship also affected me. I began to feel that I could not remain aloof from political commitment when all the people I cared for had so much more at stake than I did. Aside from the personal aspect of this decision, there are very real limitations to what one can learn about political processes through informants. If one wishes actually to watch decisions being made in a competitive political system, it is often necessary to become part of the decision-making body itself. I did this by taking highly partisan, although "behind the scenes" roles in political campaigns.

The liabilities of this strategy are numerous and deserve some attention. First, it is obvious that the more committed one is to a particular faction, the less one can learn, at first hand, about others. This may not be quite so true in higher levels of political competition where political expertise is more rationally calculated and more often bought and sold, but it is certainly the case in community politics. Even though the competition is highly institutionalized, when neighbors and workmates compete against each other, careful attention is paid to one's affiliations, and trust is easily jeopardized. In consequence of this, whenever I committed myself to a given faction I attempted to function as much as possible in capacities which would require little public exposure. In order to keep up with events in opposing factions I attempted to explain my affiliations as frankly as possible to friends on opposite sides, in much the same terms as any other resident of the community would. In this way it was possible to act as a partisan and still communicate with friends in opposing factions who acted as my informants. Here the amount of time spent in fieldwork was extremely important. I did not become actively committed until the third year of my research. By that time I had friends throughout the community who could understand, if not always agree with my partisanship.

Another problem in taking on partisan roles as a researcher is that it almost inevitably causes bias in favor of those to whom one is committed. In my case, again, the answer to this problem was to maintain close informants on opposing sides, and to try, in the analysis of events, to be on guard against my own partialities so that I might correct them or use them knowingly. It is also true that by taking on activist roles the researcher's own actions may alter the situation. Aside from the problems of analysis which this presents, it may also draw one into further commitment. For example, in becoming involved with South Chicago political leaders, and especially with unionist politicians, I began to feel responsible for the future. Once having taken an active part in political competition, I no longer felt that my relationship with the community would end when the study was completed.

The Caseworker

VICTOR AYALA

Victor Ayala teaches and counsels students at New York Technical College, a campus of the City University of New York. He has also worked for many years as a counselor to AIDS patients in a large public hospital. Out of this work came the realization that little attention has been paid to the plight of indigent patients who suffer and die on the AIDS wards of public hospitals. That plight became the subject of his book Falling Through the Cracks: AIDS and the Urban Poor, *from which this selection is taken.*

In his book and other writings, Ayala strives to demonstrate that even homeless drug addicts and other indigent victims of AIDS are human beings deserving care and compassion. As a community activist for AIDS prevention and treatment, he is a vocal advocate of measures designed to ease the suffering of AIDS patients and to help reduce the risks of infection among the residents of poor urban neighborhoods. In 1995 he was recognized for his efforts in a citation awarded to him by the President of the Borough of Brooklyn.

Ayala's study represents a growing trend toward ethnographic "action research." Ayala began working in the hospital not as a researcher but as one who wished to help ease the suffering of indigent AIDS patients. But as a graduate student in sociology, he realized that there was an urgent need for more insight and knowledge about issues in the treatment of those patients. In consequence, he began writing daily field notes about his experiences in the hospital. In time, the notes became the basis for his doctoral dissertation, and eventually for his book.

From Victor Ayala, *Falling Through the Cracks: AIDS and the Urban Poor* (Bayside, NY: Social Change Press, 1996).

The AIDS epidemic continues with little hope of a cure. The patient profile has changed over the years and an increasing number of the victims are poor minority group members with long histories of self-abuse. Firsthand accounts of the world of the indigent AIDS patient can contribute to the development of more effective strategies for treatment and prevention. Ayala provides a model for committed and informative research in the interests of indigent AIDS patients and their caregivers. Unfortunately, there is very little literature on this subject, in part because the population Ayala writes about is so highly stigmatized. In this regard, Ayala's work, like that of Claire Sterk, is an example of pioneering and quietly courageous ethnography.

The first day I entered Oremus Hospital I was shown the medical ward where I would spend the next twenty-two months. I met five patients in various stages of HIV diagnosis and AIDS-related illness. I wondered what I had gotten myself into. At first I was overwhelmed by the suffering I witnessed. During those early days I would have to leave the room in the middle of a counseling session in order to regain my composure. There were many sleepless nights as my rest was invaded by memories of patients moaning, complaining, and physically struggling with illness and death.

I didn't want to be there. I felt astonished, saddened, heartbroken at the magnitude of the illness there. I hated the sight and smell of people so distorted by disease. They moved so slowly, and the look of death was in their eyes. Some of them would not talk to me.

In time the initial shock dissipated and I focused more on my duties and responsibilities as a caseworker. After gathering the necessary demographic information and family history for the case record, I assessed each patient's social service needs and helped develop a hospital discharge plan for that patient. This required interaction with the patient and assessment of his or her understanding of the diagnosis or medical condition. This was not usually an easy process. It often took a long time to engage patients in conversation. Questions about matters of lifestyle were often perceived as invasions of privacy and viewed with great suspicion. It became clear that I needed to find ways of establishing trust and confidence with people whose lives were often characterized by desertion, betrayal, and dishonesty.

During the initial meetings it was not uncommon for patients to refuse to speak with me ("What the fuck do you want?" "Who are you?" "I don't want to be answering so many questions!"). Some people ignored me, simply pulling the sheets over their heads and hoping that I would leave the room. If they spoke, it was to ask that I turn off the lights and close the door on my way out. When I reached the point where I no longer took such rejections personally, I would take a seat, remain silent, and wait until the patient spoke. This approach often required several tries to be effective. Other times, I attempted to buy the patients' confidence by doing little favors for them—purchasing cigarettes, candy, or clothing; making telephone calls; or sometimes taking their requests to the doctors or nurses. Reports of these actions circulated among the patients, and over time I cultivated a favorable reputation ("That Ayala is OK, you can talk to him, he listens . . . [he] respects our type of people").

As a caseworker, I was exposed to the factors that these patients dealt with on a regular basis: homelessness, drug addiction, loneliness, chaotic lifestyles, and now the unfamiliar routine of hospitalization and the uncontrollable developments occurring in their bodies. Much of my counseling time was spent encouraging the patients to speak about their lives and their understanding of AIDS. It was important for me to be genuine, empathic, and honest about caring for them and wanting to make their hospital experience easier. Because most were homeless, intravenous drug users, sex workers, criminals of various kinds, or homosexuals, and sometimes various combinations of these, they were unaccustomed to sharing their experiences with anyone who listened in a nonjudgmental fashion. Even if they believed that I was there to help, they were often curious about my motives. I always told them that I was a caseworker; sometimes I mentioned that I was a graduate student in sociology.

There is a thin line between empathy and overidentification, and being "tested" by patients clarified this issue for me. I was always at risk of being used by patients or manipulated into actions that could sometimes prove harmful to them in the long run. This was particularly true of the substance abusers, who routinely tried to badger, beg, or cajole me into obtaining larger doses of methadone for them. At first I would rush to the nurses' station in order to accommodate the patient. Fortunately, the more experienced members of the staff and certain situations involving individual patients helped me realize that the patients' behavior was manipulative and reflected poor impulse control or pain intolerance rather than genuine need. Moreover, my lack of experience in this area created friction with the medical staff. Some of the doctors and nurses perceived my intervention on behalf of patients as an attempt to impose my judgment on theirs.

The patients had great difficulty coping with the emotions surrounding their fears of the illness and their mortality. The counseling sessions were often intense and physically draining, and as I was both caseworker and researcher, they required a serious commitment of time and energy. Being available both physically and emotionally to the patients and their families was challenging; it was also a spiritual awakening. It became clear that my reflection on the issues of death and dying was necessary, indeed unavoidable, if I was to provide any assistance to patients going through the dying process. Crossing the line from caseworker to fellow human being and back became less mechanical with each encounter.

Because the number of patients exceeded the capacity and resources of the hospital and neighborhood social services, I was in a state of continual frustration. I felt that my efforts were useless in the face of the patients' deteriorating health and imminent death. The magnitude of their psychosocial, medical, financial, and political deficits brought to the landscape of my interaction a sense of powerlessness. Simply knowing that my shift would soon be finished was a help. At other times absenteeism was the only way I could cope with my anger and depression. As time went by I had to make a concerted, conscious effort to distance myself emotionally from the patients' pain in order to minimize my own. Objectivity was the only way to deliver the best possible service at the lowest personal cost.

After a discussion with a fellow social worker I wrote the following notes:

> On this ward I deal with twenty-eight patients. It's difficult. I have to document everything that I'm doing with them. Hey, we're short staffed; could you imagine trying to be on top of the histories and personal circumstances of every one of these patients? I mean, this one is homeless, that one is a drug addict, the other one has AIDS and won't face it. You have the doctors always pushing you to find housing for patients . . . they want them OUT. So they see you in the halls and yell, "Hey, did you find housing for so and so?" We're just so short staffed; sometimes I just can't handle this. I don't know how I do this.
>
> Boy, so many people are dying up here, it's like a dying club. Sometimes I can't believe it. I just need to get out of here. I'm transferring to the ER. At least in there the patients keep moving; they come in and move out.

Eventually I found that I needed to make mental notes of the specific ways in which I helped each patient in order to feel good about the job. I focused on simply being present, listening, providing emotional support, and touching patients as concrete ways of easing their pain and fear of death. Acknowledging the validity of their lives, encouraging them to cease dwelling on the past and live each day as best they could was difficult, but it was essential both to their well-being and to mine. I made a point of observing demonstrations of commitment, even heroism on the part of co-workers. It was important to celebrate the fact the glass was half full rather than half empty.

Time proved to be a finite resource. I was never sure that there would be enough of it to uncover the needed research information or adequately serve each patient's needs. It was not uncommon for a patient to become incapacitated or to die with my work unfinished. I could not help those patients verbalize their understanding of the diagnosis, finalize discharge plans, or arrange for their last meetings with their families.

My increasing weariness and occasional depression forced me to dissociate myself emotionally from the job from time to time. I concentrated on being more professional in the execution of my duties. I became more savvy to the maneuvering of "hustlers" disguising their requests as real expressions of need. Growing to understand the background and nature of the patients enabled me to distinguish a patient participating in a bona fide methadone program from one who simply wanted the drug.

The issue of drug addiction has special implications for caseworkers. There is poor communication and, hence, little cooperation among drug treatment facilities, community-based organizations, and the hospital. It is difficult to discern what type of care is provided to patients both before and after hospitalization. Certain information cannot be obtained from other facilities because it is held confidential either by custom or under the law. Caseworkers therefore have to rely on the patients for information, and their lack of knowledge and communication skills makes it difficult to provide comprehensive medical or social service. The fact that patients frequently move from one clinic, drug treatment program, or hospital to another heightens the confusion and results in fragmented, sporadic care.

Social workers are called upon to convince patients to be more cooperative. This may be accomplished by increasing their understanding of their medical condition while addressing the myriad social conditions affecting their lives. The social worker takes on the role of advocate for the patient, attempting to sensitize physicians and nurses to the nonmedical issues affecting the patient's life. Although the social worker gains the trust and cooperation of the patient, the doctor–patient relationship does not necessarily improve. To some extent, an adversary relationship—us versus them—develops between the staff and the patients.

The attitudes of staff members at Oremus Hospital were condescending at times. They tended to blame the victim, believing that the patients' illnesses were their own fault ("If they didn't do what they're doing, they wouldn't have AIDS." "If they'd follow my directions, they'd be outta here!"). They also had a poor attitude toward the caseworker. Such attitudes were expressed when a doctor would interrupt a counseling session, discounting my presence and invalidating my work, sometimes acting as if I wasn't even there. One intern interrupted a session and instructed me not to allow the patient "to cry and get out of control." He insisted that I focus on helping the patient understand the medical procedure and the diagnosis. Ironically, I was doing just that, but with his clinical blinders on he was unable to see that the expression of emotion could serve as a means of attaining greater understanding. Another incident occurred at a time when a patient was near death. As I held her hand and attempted to reassure and comfort her as she passed through this most fearful of moments, a doctor abruptly came in to draw blood. Despite his awareness of the patient's condition, he could not separate himself from his clinical routine even for a moment.

Despite the negative attitudes of some staff members, I was usually able to convince them of the need for more attention for patients who were truly in need. I learned how to approach the staff with unusual requests. I also learned to respect the staff's work habits and accepted the fact that they are the ones who decide when patients will be seen and the medical treatments they will receive.

Conversely, the physicians and nurses relied on me to identify the patients' social service needs. It was my function to clarify the medical issues for the patient and his or her family, if any. I was responsible for the development and implementation of discharge plans so as to avoid unnecessarily long hospital stays. In the best of circumstances, this proved advantageous for both the patient and the hospital. But in too many cases the lack of appropriate housing, supportive counseling, community-based referrals, or other services would leave patients to fend for themselves once they were discharged from the hospital.

Discharge proved especially difficult for the homeless patients. Patients with confirmed AIDS diagnoses were not accepted by local shelters. This was a source of considerable friction between the hospital administrators and doctors and the caseworkers and neighborhood social service organizations. Battles over turf or areas of professional responsibility could easily leave patients without adequate care.

The staff was placed in the awkward position of withholding information about a patient's HIV-positive or AIDS status from family members or friends if the patient so desired. Many of the patients willingly informed friends or family of their diagnosis, but generally this occurred only after several counseling sessions. In some instances the caseworker was asked to be present at the time of the revelation. There were too many cases in which wives, lovers, or pregnant girlfriends could not be told the truth about a patient's status because the patient refused to reveal it. Fear of rejection or embarrassment, or simply irresponsibility, kept patients from sharing this information with those who had a right to know. In potentially life-threatening situations moral persuasion was applied; nevertheless, in too many instances the news was revealed after the patient's demise. Then the medical, nursing, and social service staff was left to cope with the outrage of friends or family members.

A patient I was working with introduced me to his wife, who had recently had one child and was two months pregnant. He did not want her to know that he had AIDS. During my conversation with her she said that he had told her he had pneumonia. Despite much dialogue he resisted telling her the truth. The doctors and I decided that if he did not tell her, we would. Later the wife was informed and underwent HIV antibody testing. Although I was pleased with this development, I was struck by the husband's degree of control over the situation.

I was able to contain my fear of exposure by keeping in mind the information circulated by the CDC about modes of HIV transmission. I was more concerned about susceptibility to airborne bacteria expelled by patients with rare, but more or less contagious, diseases such as salmonella, tuberculosis, meningitis, chicken pox, and herpes simplex. Complicating the issue further was the observation that neither the patients nor the staff always abided by established precautionary guidelines. I began to fear contagion from less-than-vigilant co-workers. I took precautions, but the more time I spent at the hospital, the more concerned I became about the possibility of infection.

In the end, the need to continue my work overshadowed my fear of contagion. The patients needed someone to serve as a link between their desolate existence and people who could provide some comfort. Even the healthcare workers, however entrenched they were in medical procedures, continued to serve. Perhaps one can assume that they did so merely to maintain their livelihood. But when nurses came in day after day and donned protective clothing, caring for patient after patient, one cannot dismiss the thought that perhaps they felt the pangs of humanity and did their jobs because they experienced the rewards of merging medical treatment with human understanding.

Part IV

The Observer's Role

Researching Peasants and Drug Producers

EDMUNDO MORALES

The Peruvian-born sociologist Edmundo Morales has conducted extensive research on narcotics and substance abuse, with particular emphasis on cocaine production and trafficking. In 1983 he decided to return to his native region in the Andes Mountains to explore the changes that had occurred there as a result of the shift of the local economy toward the production and processing of cocaine for export. For cocaine and its derivatives, often known as "white gold," have become the drugs of the 1980s, and in Peru the new cocaine economy has displaced the former Andean coca trade.

In the course of his research, Morales discovered that the peasants of the Andes villages had become dependent on the worldwide traffic in cocaine. Most of them worked for several months each year in coca-processing laboratories hidden in the jungle. Others sold meat to the managers of the cocaine factories. Morales was dismayed to see so much food being diverted to the jungles from the impoverished highlands. Although the peasants were gaining cash income, they were also becoming addicted to cocaine and were ignoring the need for more important social changes in their own villages.

The purpose of Morales's study was to identify alternative means of making a living for peasants who support themselves by participating in the cocaine economy. To do so, Morales needed to analyze the social, cultural, economic, and political meaning of the cocaine industry—an immense task, despite his knowledge of the Quechua language and his familiarity with the culture of the people he was study-

This selection is adapted from Edmundo Morales, *Cocaine: White Gold Rush in Peru* (Tucson: University of Arizona Press, 1989).

ing. He spent several summers visiting and interviewing the people of the highlands, often experiencing unexpected hardships.. Some of those hardships are described in this selection from his book, Cocaine: White Gold Rush in Peru, *which was published in 1989. The selection also addresses the issues and dangers confronting a researcher who is observing people engaging in illegal activities.*

During a visit to my hometown in the spring of 1980, I decided to do what a professor in college had advised me: "Go back home and look into the changes in the community." Neither during my childhood nor in numerous visits back had I ventured outside the boundaries of my native community, Llamellín. In my youth, I was part of the indigenous culture and, as an adult visitor, I lacked the skills to make sense of the obvious. Becoming an ethnographer of the Andes, native though I was, was a long process, for learning from or observing other people whose culture and society is the same as one's own roots I found very difficult and possible only when a disciplined approach was incorporated into my everyday routine.

On my exploratory trip in 1980, the first thing I did when I arrived in the district capital of Llamellín was to look for a companion who was familiar with the route and the area. A local photographer volunteered for the trip. The next step was to rent a horse or a mule for transportation, and prepare a *fiambre,* provision consisting of two guinea pigs, toasted maize, and some homemade bread for at least two days' travel. My companion and I left town and headed for Paras, the community of my first fieldwork.

After thirteen hours of tedious horseback riding, we followed the recommendation of a teacher we had met on our way and stopped in one of the five villages of Paras. At the church of San Martín, we washed our hands and watered our horses. Directly across from the church was a house with Coca-Cola posters on the door. We knocked on the door but there was no answer. Through the next door of the same house we heard voices. Someone noticed us and came out to ask what we wanted. He was drunk. We told him that we only wanted a bottle of Coca-Cola, to which he answered that all he had was alcohol and alcohol was as good as cold water. We had run out of boiled drinking water and had to try to find something to satisfy our thirst. He asked our names and we asked his. We found out that he was the lieutenant governor *(teniente gobernador)* for the five villages of Paras. Assuming that he would use his influence, we asked him to recommend someone in the community to give us shelter for at least one night. He went into the room where the rest of his friends were discussing their plans. Shortly thereafter six drunken peasants stood before us.

They introduced themselves by their titles. They were the members of the central committee of the community. Each of them asked us questions about our identity, profession, and especially the purpose of our visit to Paras. They wanted me to show them some kind of letter of introduction or at least a personal identification card bearing my picture and my name, or even a calling card from any provincial authority introducing me to the community. I had nothing, not even my school identification card. I explained my presence and purposes to them over and over and begged them to believe me. They would not accept the excuse that I had left all my documents in Llamellín, nor would they believe that I had been born and raised in the province.

Since I could not provide identification, they asked us "kindly and immediately" to leave the village. It was getting dark and we had nowhere to go. Suddenly the president of the Administrative Council addressed my companion and said, "I think I know you." My companion presented his identification as a photographer, but I remained a problem. They invited us to have a drink before leaving the village and we accepted. My companion and I drank the alcohol, smiling and looking at the Coca-Cola poster. At this point I asked the peasants to let me take their picture. They liked the idea of posing as members of the central committee. Almost in unison they said, "Yes, my engineer." Then they wanted me to pose with them for another frame. Right after my assistant snapped the camera, I suggested we have another drink and offered to pay for it. "Correct, my engineer," they answered. By the time we had emptied the bottle we all were friends, and the same person who had asked us to leave the village offered us his humble home for as long as we wanted to stay in Paras. He hoped it would be a long stay.

The Solis family gave us the best room they had, which apparently had been unoccupied for some time. We used the only steel bedstead they had. Our bed linen consisted of four sheepskins and two wool quilts infested with fleas and lice which made our nights interminable. One day before we left the village the Solis family killed a pig to give us a farewell lunch. They assigned us their best mules for our transportation back to Llamellín and one of them even walked for about one hour with us up to the point where the broad trail began that would make our return easier.

Aside from the first day of difficulty, I had no problem at all as a visitor in Paras. There was some hesitation when I presented myself as a sociology graduate student from New York and spoke to them in Quechua. However, as they listened to me speaking to them in terms that only a native could understand, telling them jokes and fairy tales, they gave broad smiles as a sign of accepting their visitor. From then on, they acted friendly and were responsive and cooperative. I entered their lives and functioned almost as one of them. Good humor, patience, and the bottle of alcohol spent on the first day produced excellent returns.

*   *   *

In the spring of 1981, about one month before my trip from New York, I asked the chairperson of my committee to sign a letter in Spanish addressed to the head of the police, the subprefecto, the mayor, the judge of First Instance, and the director of education of the Province. In Lima, I obtained a letter of introduction from the American Embassy wherein the cultural attache stated the purpose of my stay in Peru; this letter opened the doors of public libraries (there are not many of them), universities, museums, and so forth.

Once in the capital town of the province to which Paras belongs, I paid formal visits to the authorities to whom the letter from my mentor had been directed. The authorities, in turn, had already sent a transcription of the letter to their representatives in other towns announcing my presence and asking them for cooperation in the research.

When I arrived in Illauro, the village of my residence during fieldwork, the local teacher whom I had met a year before was expecting me. He had already rented a one-room house for me near the school building where he lived. He had my room cleaned by his students and borrowed a bedstead, sheepskins, quilts, and a table from various families. I had taken my own sleeping bag. Despite my experience the year before with lice and fleas, I failed to bring with me any insecticides, so pediculosis was inevitable.

The next morning I was having breakfast when a delegation of authorities from the village of San Martín came to welcome me and, at the same time, invite me once again to live in their village. I explained to them that I had not come exclusively to spend my time in Illauro or any of the five villages. I said I would be visiting every family I could, and that the only reason I had settled in Illauro was that the local teacher had rented a house for me there. When they knew the location of my house, which lay about twenty-five steps from a young, attractive widow's house, they smiled, wished me luck, and left.

The first person I had planned to visit was the village leader who, during my previous visit, had offered me full cooperation and who I thought would be my key informant. He had changed his mind and refused to cooperate. He advised me to pick another community to avoid problems with the local people. He had secretly started warning his co-villagers of the danger of my presence in Paras owing to my "identification with the other party." He also urged them to expel me from the community, for I had no official authorization to stay in Paras. He did not know that I had been authorized by the provincial authorities to do research, and he was surprised when he learned that I had been cleared in every respect. My research project became more and more challenging.

It had first been my plan to collect historical and political data, but as a result of the visit to the leader I decided to start immediately interviewing and observing the people. No one resisted. Fortunately, when I went back to Llamellín after staying two weeks in Paras, I met an Aprista congressman visiting the province who had already been informed of my project. The congressman asked me to join him at a lunch where he was to be a guest of the notables of Llamellín. After lunch, while we were still talking, the leader who had tried to create difficulties for me knocked on the door. He came to urge the congressman to visit Paras. The lawmaker took the opportunity to ask him his reasons for refusing to cooperate with my endeavor and pleaded with him to change his attitude.

*   *   *

In any direct contact with the observed population, the researcher perhaps enters the field under the aegis of an official agency or as a social scientist directly identifying himself as such. In the present research, I took the second alternative. Any official sponsorship could have created serious difficulties because of the conflict existing among the members of the community, as well as their hostile attitude toward the government.

During the process of data gathering as a participant observer, I became a temporary member of the community without identifying with any of the political groups, thus avoiding a dual identity. I visited three to five families per day; I spent the rest of the day talking with shepherds and workers in the fields or taking notes. I conducted the interviews in Quechua in order to make the people feel comfortable and to facilitate a better and more precise expression of their feelings, opinions, attitudes, and ideas. I would always start conversations with flattering statements to elicit a discussion or a friendly argument. For example, I would approach a shepherd girl or a woman on her land by saying "you have such a large herd," or "you look beautiful on your plot," to which they would always answer by telling stories of their past or by comparing their land possession to that of some families who they thought had more land than they needed.

Sometimes people would avoid the question and ask the reason for my stay in the area. I would tell women that I was in "search of a girl to marry," and this led to questions of their marital status, number of children, size of land, and so forth. Male peasants like conversations involving women, so I would approach them by asking whether there was any "available girl in the community, for everyone says that they are all yours; why do you not leave one for a poor guy like myself?" Some would name the single women or just smile at me. Others would bounce the question and say, "Why would you want another woman when you already have your blonde widow?" This approach worked much better than just knocking on doors with a long questionnaire in hand and saying: "Hi, I am doing research on peasant economy and would like you to answer some questions."

The purpose of the research had been to study the effects of land reform and modernization in the peasant community of Paras. A basic questionnaire designed to obtain data on the demographic, social, and economic aspects of the community was taken to the field. In the process of my visits and interviews I discovered that, right after the harvest, some peasants started making preparations for a long trip. Thus, my plan had to be changed. It needed to fit what was going in the field, which was different from what I had expected. After discovering the new research material, I centered my efforts on the *mantanero* peasants and some informants in small towns in the area. The reason informal conversations with indirect questions were formulated was that peasants are very sensitive to direct questions about themselves.

After defending my dissertation, I spent most of the summer of 1983 in Peru. The purposes of the trip were to study more closely the peasants of Paras who were connected to the underground economy, to make some exploratory visits to coca- and cocaine-producing communities, and to try to meet and become acquainted with experts in the industry.

My trip to the drug-plagued communities made many people think that I was a *pichicatero* (drug trafficker). On more than one occasion they offered me certain amounts of the "best stuff," but I cautiously avoided both too much information and direct or indirect involvement in drug trafficking. My cautious attitude owed to my suspicion that a trap had been set by local drug lords, many of whom had been my grade-school friends, high-school classmates, and fellow factory workers in Lima. Although to the people in the Andes I was continuing to do research on the changes in traditional communities, some suspected I was interested in something else. However, to them, that "something else" was not research but "white business."

My aluminum camera case was always the first thing to be searched at every police checkpoint. In many communities people thought that I was a foreigner. They whispered to each other in Quechua, saying "God knows what this *Colombiano* carries in that shiny case." Situations like this were opportunities to start conversations about drug production and traffic. Socializing with people at every level was my basic method of research. The disadvantage of this strategy is that it is time-consuming and limited to researchers with a deep knowledge of native language and culture.

*   *   *

On a bus I met two migrant workers from a village near my hometown who were coming back from the Upper Huallaga. They supplied the first details I had obtained on the preparation of coca paste. Three peasants from Paras not only provided the names and exact locations of research settings but also were willing to go with me to the jungles. A local teacher from a highland village who was taking a leave of absence to work on the coca plantations also became part of my direct connections to the underworld.

I traveled north to the hamlet where my friend the teacher was working. All I had were the names of the teacher's relatives, the nearby village, and a piece of paper giving vague directions. Despite the fact that I had asked the driver and his helper to drop me at the place where I had been told to get off, I missed my stop by about two kilometers. I got off at a place where about ten people were picking coca leaves, and I walked back until I found the right house. Neither my friend the teacher nor his relatives were home. The man in charge of the small hardware store was very apathetic toward me. When I asked him about the owner of the house, he brusquely answered, "He is not in."

My hosts introduced me to the area residents as one of their relatives from Lima visiting them for a few weeks. I spent the first days of fieldwork socializing. As days passed, I got deeper and deeper into the underground economy and subculture, avoiding direct questions regarding formulas, proportions, procedures, and prices. I participated in every routine or special event I could and observed others. For example, after a volleyball game among local residents, I sat and had refreshments with the neighbors who usually asked about my plans for the next day. I was always open to suggestions and invitations to visit their plantations or their farmhouses deep in the forests. Often, the trips involved hours of hiking, especially when the visits were to secret airfields.

Following a successful stay, I would move to other sites. The strategy was always to produce networks of friendship. But I never went anywhere without actually knowing the setting and the host families. This meant many hours of traveling, by car, bus, truck, or on foot. My peasant friends from Paras helped me cross passes and mountain ranges to reach areas that did not have road service. They always made jokes about my limited physical endurance. For the longer hikes, my traveling equipment consisted of my worn-out sleeping bag, a small tin pot in which to boil water, some matches, basic medicines, my 35-millimeter camera, and many rolls of film. Hunger and thirst made us drop in on communities or isolated houses during the treks across the mountain ranges. Under the pretext of having the peasant women cook our meals, we stopped overnight in houses and huts where friends or acquaintances of my peasant hiking experts lived. Questions such as "What brings you here?" and "Where are you from?" were constantly addressed to me. To them, I was from Llamellín, my hometown. Some peasants, especially males, tested me with their questions. My responses never failed to reassure them about my identity.

The actual recording of data varied according to the conditions in the settings, types of subjects, and kinds of information needed. Days in the highlands are short and the majority of people do not have electricity. Wax candles, kerosene lanterns, and flashlights are used by those who can afford them. I therefore made field notes immediately following interviews and conversations during the day. Evenings and nights were usually spent chatting with neighbors in my village of residence. Thus, the apparent physical disadvantage of the setting turned into an advantage. Evening and night conversations and discussions were ways to double-check information I had collected.

I gathered data on coca-leaf economy, costs and process of manufacturing, and national and international trafficking of coca paste and cocaine at different places in the country. Knowledge of every aspect of the underground hustle and bustle came from direct observation and participation. As I had good rapport with the people, some days I would ask them to let me drop in to their work settings. Then I would show up with a couple of bottles of beer, Coca-Cola, or anything that would season my visit. During the first visits, I tried not to be too inquisitive, for I perceived tension in some individuals, especially the full-time cocaine entrepreneurs. As had happened in the highlands in 1980, patience and good humor paid good returns.

*   *   *

The study, besides being an intellectual and an academic endeavor, was an opportunity for photographic expression. If my two native tongues, Quechua and Spanish, were extremely valuable during data collection, my photographic skills were equally important. Since my first visits to my hometown in the mid-1970s, I have been photographing the people and the culture of the Andes. Hundreds of exposures of color slides document my presence and knowledge of the Andean countries at large. The visual side of the research in and of itself represents a whole new dimension of social research. However, a camera hanging on the researcher's neck can be potentially dangerous when people do not want to be photographed and sometimes brought me rejection, disappointment, and setbacks.

In 1973, during my first visit to my hometown from New York, I wanted to photograph the people from a nearby village. I found two peasant shepherd boys who seemed to make an interesting picture. I aimed my camera mounted with a long telephoto lens. One of the children realized that I was snapping the camera. The boys started screaming and throwing stones at me. A few minutes later, parents and neighbors came out with their dogs, sticks, and more stones. They thought that I had been trying to shoot the children with a gun. On another occasion during fieldwork in 1981, a peasant asked me to use my camera to see whether there was underground water in the mountains surrounding the community.

If in the Andes my nightly research companion was a cassette recorder, during the day my camera was the research associate always hanging on my shoulder, ready to freeze segments and instants of what was happening in the community. However, photographing and taping subjects raises the ethical question of whether or not the participants in the research should be made aware of the use of audiovisual devices during research contact. Many Andean populations are sensitive to having their voices taped or their images recorded on film. The experiences noted earlier made me more cautious in the taping and photographing I did afterwards.

Strangers carrying cameras are not yet seen in the cocaine towns and villages, because there is no such thing as tourists or visitors taking snapshots of farms and landscapes or posing with natives for a souvenir photo. In the underground world, nobody wants to be photographed regardless of his status. Obviously, not everyone toting a camera is a journalist. On the other hand, there is no way for the illegal world to know whether an occasional visitor is a drug spy or an undercover law-enforcement agent. They suspect that anyone taking pictures of them working is an enemy. This may be one of the reasons why photographs or films that reach our attention have almost always been taken under police protection or as part of a crackdown or a drug bust. These kinds of photographs and films are more sensational and biased. Lack of respect and consideration for the subject breaks the interrelationship between the photographer and his subject. Furthermore, the police seem to be oriented toward showing how excellent the control and eradication programs are or publicizing widespread drug abuse.

On the last day of my stay in the green mines, I decided to take some pictures of a busy Sunday in one of the cocaine centers. When a peasant friend and I were walking around the main square taking candid shots of migrant workers, three men approached us. They pointed at me and said, "You are an outsider, aren't you?" Then they asked whether my cameras were for sale. I replied no. They all deliberated briefly. They asked me at which hotel I was staying. I gave the name of a low-class hotel. Their advice was that I should leave town immediately. They showed me the park bench where two reporters had been shot to death a few feet from where I was standing and emphasized their advice by saying, "If you don't pack and leave the town immediately you'll be another statistic; so if you want to live longer than twenty-four hours, get the hell out of here."

I thanked them for their advice and expressed my gratitude for their concern. I accepted the glass of beer they invited me to drink. Isn't life full of hellos and good-byes? What had happened to me in the highlands in 1980 was repeated at the other end of my research. This time, however, rather than trying to make friends as I had done in the highlands, I put my gear away, walked around the square, and left the town.

The Fieldworker and
the Surgeon

CHARLES BOSK

For eighteen months Charles Bosk was a participant observer in the surgical train-ing program at a large teaching hospital. His research was designed to explore three themes: social control (how does the medical profession evaluate and control the behavior of its members?); social support (how do physicians control the perfor-mance of subordinates yet allow them room to make honest errors?); and dealing with failure (how do surgeons cope with the knowledge that their errors sometimes cause suffering and death?).

"Pacific Hospital," where Bosk conducted his research, is an elite teaching insti-tution surrounded by a lower-class neighborhood whose residents often seek medical care at the hospital's emergency room. The surgical staff at Pacific Hospital must treat many patients who are in extreme pain, often as a result of traumas such as gunshot wounds or stabbings. Thus, the surgeons must often work under condi-tions that are far from ideal, making errors more likely.

Bosk was permitted to observe the operations of two surgical services, focusing on the ways in which errors are detected, evaluated, and corrected. He followed sur-geons through their daily activities: visiting patients twice daily on rounds; drink-ing coffee in the doctors' lounge during time-out periods; assisting on operations when hands were short; standing by when bodies were pronounced dead; staying

Parts of this selection are adapted from Charles Bosk, *Forgive and Remember: Managing Medical Failure.* Copyright © 1979 by The University of Chicago. Abridgment © 1989 by The University of Chicago. All rights reserved. Adapted with permission of The University of Chicago Press. The last part of this selection is from "The Fieldworker as Watcher and Witness," *Hastings Center Report* 15, no. 3. (Hastings-on-Hudson, N.Y.: Society of Ethics and Life Sciences, June 1985).

on call at night. He became aware of the shared world view of the members of the surgical work group, the way they judge themselves and others, and their attitudes toward patients. He found that resident surgeons are forgiven if they make mistakes that the older surgeons believe to be "normal" aspects of the learning process. They are not forgiven, however, when their mistakes are repeated or are thought to be due to carelessness.

In this selection Bosk describes many of the issues that must be confronted by researchers working in delicate situations in which confidentiality is absolutely essential.

As I reflect on the experience of eighteen months of participant observation in a teaching hospital, and on the dilemmas of the observer role, I feel a sense of respect for data-collecting procedures which allow the researcher to keep the sensuous world at a distance, and which thereby allow him to avoid the self-exposure, self-reflection, and self-doubt endemic to fieldworkers. In the field, the everyday life of his subjects overwhelms the researcher, threatens to obliterate his sense of self, and forces a reconsideration of deeply held personal and intellectual beliefs. It would be of little point, then, for me to pretend that I was merely a coding machine which transcribed the events of everyday life into field material. Instead, I would like to describe the field experience itself.

How did I begin? The first thing I did was to approach an attending [physician] I had met at a party, explain my proposed study, and ask for his cooperation. The attending expressed enthusiasm for the project, but refused his cooperation. He claimed that if I wanted to really be trusted, I would need the housestaff's acceptance. He expressed his fear that his sponsorship would be a "kiss of death": Housestaff would view me as his spy and never talk freely with me. If I wanted my project to succeed, he advised, I needed to be seen as my own person. So rather than somehow magically start the research, he gave me the names of a number of residents.

Not sure if I was receiving aid or a runaround from my initial contact, I called the first name on his list, the chief resident. We met for coffee and I explained my plans. The resident approved my being an observer on his service, but claimed he would have to check with both attendings. The chairman of my department provided a letter of introduction to the chairman of the Department of Surgery. Gaining my initial entree was a multistaged diplomatic problem. Each interaction was a test, and access was the result of continual testing and retesting. Entree was not something negotiated once and then over and done with.

Access—being allowed in the scene—is one thing, but approval and trust of field subjects is quite another. Much is made in fieldwork accounts of the "cover story" which the observer uses to explain his presence in the setting as a first and essential step in gaining trust. My cover story was very simple. I explained that I was doing a dissertation on the way surgeons learned to recognize and control error. The surgeons were, as a rule, remarkably uncurious about my research. None ever questioned the legitimacy of my research question or the nature of my methods during our initial meetings. Few even requested that I account for my presence. I was not asked for my cover story very often and, when asked for the story, I was not required to elaborate on it. In some sense, my access was secured by sponsorship of housestaff trusted by all. Once my access was established, my cover story was superfluous.

Trust was gained neither during initial introductions nor by the artful manipulation of a cover story, but through my performance in roles I assumed and was assigned by housestaff and attendings. Housestaff assigned me a number of roles. Most generally, I was an "extra pair of hands" and a "gofer." During the time of my fieldwork, I became very proficient at opening packages of bandages, retrieving charts, and fetching items from the supply room. Through these tasks, I expressed some solidarity with whatever group I was observing and gave something, however inconsequential, in exchange for "observing rights."

Second, I was an "emissary from the outside world." My round of life was less circumscribed than a houseofficer's: I read and watched more news, saw more movies, and participated more fully in university life outside the hospital. In some sense, I provided housestaff contact with a world they felt cut off from. During Watergate, I always brought a number of papers into the hospital. How or why this became my task I do not know. Often I purchased these papers at the hospital gift stand, a place interns and residents certainly had access to. Their general reluctance to pick such papers up is not so much a mark of their frugality as a symbolic statement about their relation to the world outside Pacific Hospital. I later learned that housestaff attach a magical property to newspapers, books, and magazines. If they bring them in to work they see this as jinxing themselves and condemning the group to an impossible, busy day. It is, however, permissible for outsiders to bring such taboo items to them. My passing remarks about movies, current events, the weather—all were taken as an indication of what educated people on the outside were thinking.

Third, I was a "fellow-sufferer." As a graduate student not released from training, I was perceived as occupying a position analogous to the houseofficer's. My own career problems and expectations were topics that houseofficers initiated much conversation about. They constantly compared and contrasted our different experiences. During such exchanges, houseofficers constantly emphasized the indignity of their roles and often suggested that their present burdens justified their future rewards. From me, they sought to learn about the generalized indignities of the subordinate role in sociological training. I regaled them with my wildest recollections of coding data and proofreading galleys.

Fourth, I was a convenient "sounding board." I was surprised at the degree that informants sought me out to relate stories of practice that they disagreed with. Feelings that were not shared in the group, discontents, uncertainties were taken to me. I knew that observers were often sought by organizational malcontents; what surprised me was that all my informants were at one time or another malcontents. Disfiguring palliative operations, patient discomfort, and the openness of communications among the ranks were the most common complaints. As a "sounding board," I was implicitly asked to play a quasi-therapeutic role: to listen without judging and to understand.

Fifth, houseofficers viewed me as a "referee" in conflicts among themselves over patient management, quarrels over the equity of the division of labor, and disputes about whether or not patients understood what was happening. In the midst of such disagreements, one houseofficer would turn to me and ask: "Well, what do you think? Which of us is right?" These were not comfortable situations for me when I could hide behind the observer role. A judgment was demanded as the price for my continued presence. Moreover, any judgment was certain to alienate one of my informants. I developed tactics for throwing the question back to the disputants or for pointing out the merits of either side, or making a joke of the entire dispute. Over time, I tried in vain to teach my subjects that such conflict resolution was not a proper part of my role. Nevertheless, being asked to referee disputes was a recurrent and always problematic task and not one that I ever felt totally comfortable with. As I felt more accepted, I was somewhat better able to put questions off. But in the beginning, I was stiff, uncomfortable, and always mindful of my relationships with each party.

Sixth, I was the group "historian." Because of the way housestaff rotate through the various services, it was not unusual for me to have been on a given service longer than any particular houseofficer. When this occurred, I was expected to know something of the history of the different patients on the service. I was expected to keep track of attendings' remarks and verify them for absent group members. The role of group historian served me well, since it forced housestaff to depend on me for information that they needed. This created a greater sense of mutual obligation between housestaff and myself and to the degree that the information I supplied was reliable, I established my credibility. Also, I was a short-run as well as long-run historian. I would often ask housestaff about action that I could not watch but was interested in. On more than one occasion, my questioning reminded houseofficers of a task that had until then slipped their minds. My unwitting reminders saved them from over-sights which would have gotten them into trouble. The fact that such incidents occurred further indebted housestaff to me and heightened my legitimacy. A fieldworker pays a price for this kind of legitimacy, though. The historian role itself presents some of the most common moral dilem-mas that a fieldworker faces. Each time I gave such a reminder to a house-officer, I changed what would have otherwise happened without this in-tervention. Lab tests, consultations with other physicians, and conferences with patients and their families—all these were on occasion events that took place because I reminded houseofficers of them. By jogging the memory of houseofficers in this way, I made it impossible for myself to observe what happens when these events fail to occur.

Despite the fact that it was not my intention in these instances to change the action I was studying, one can see very clearly that errors of omission present the observer with a moral dilemma. If one does remind a houseofficer, one disturbs by that act the very relationships one is at-tempting to study. However, if one does not remind the houseofficer—and yet knows he has overlooked something—it is possible that a patient's care will be compromised. In most cases when I asked if something had been done, I did so because as a sociologist I was particularly interested in seeing or hearing a report of that specific action, and usually because I was unaware of whether it had occurred or not—I was trying to orient myself. If the houseofficer had forgotten about the task I was asking about, if it had completely slipped his mind, then that fact told me some-thing about the difference between a sociological perspective and a surgi-cal one; and I learned something more about the structure of the sur-geon's life-world.

If errors of omission present observers with one type of moral dilemma, errors of commission present him with another. In the case where the fieldworker knows that some harm has been done to a patient through physician or nursing error, does the observer have any direct, ethical obli-gations to the patient and his/her family? That is, should the fieldworker either inform the patient or find some alternative means of making pub-lic the error? I chose not to do this for a variety of reasons. As a pragmatic matter, being a patient-advocate would have made the kind of fieldwork I wanted to do impossible. Moreover, I felt a responsibility to other medical sociologists who wished to undertake field projects in the future. I was aware that my conduct could either make the way more or less difficult for those who followed me. While some participant-observer effects seem acceptable to me, others, those that contravene the basic operating norms of a group, are not acceptable. These larger effects not only distort the phenomenon under study, they make it impossible for later fieldworkers to gain access to and legitimacy within medical settings. Most important,

I felt I could discharge my ethical obligations to patients more effectively by describing the general categorization and management of error rather than tilting at windmills in one or two select cases.

Whatever roles houseofficers cast me in or I assumed, the major irony of the fieldworker role was always apparent: On the one hand, I was intimately involved in all aspects of the everyday life of a group; and on the other hand, I was constrained by the nature of my task to exert as little social influence in that group as possible. So, my sensitivity to the group's actions and their consequences was heightened at the same time that my theoretic commitments restrained me from even raising the group's consciousness about the effects of its own actions.

I had less intimate contact with attendings than with housestaff, and assumed and was assigned a narrower range of roles. Most commonly, I was seen as any other "medical student." Attendings assimilated me to the group by treating me like any other member of the group. They had me look down proctoscopy tubes, rake abdomens feeling for a mass, and learn to hold retractors properly. Their treatment of me helped strengthen my ties to houseofficers, who saw that not only was I not in league with attendings, but that, like them, I was the occasional butt of an attending's sense of humor. By the same token, my own willingness to take part this way in group life served notice to attendings that I was willing to do what was necessary to complete my project. When attendings viewed me as a medical student, they often tried to teach me concise medical lessons. Whatever problems of identification and rapport I might have had, it is interesting to note that attendings had some of their own. Toward the end of my fieldwork, two attendings approached me, told me that I must be interested in medicine to have spent so much time at Pacific Hospital, and then informed me that if I wanted to go to medical school, they would help me in any way they could. I took their offer as an indication that perhaps I had been in the field long enough.

The incident above is related to another role attendings cast me in—their "advisee." Attendings offered two types of advice. First, there was "scientific" advice. Here attendings would address themselves to the design of my study. They wanted to know about my control groups, my measurement instruments, my hypotheses, and all similar paraphernalia from the type of research they engaged in. When I would explain that my model for research was somewhat different from theirs, they were skeptical but generally tolerant. After all, I was the sociology department's problem, and not theirs. Second, attendings offered "interpretive advice." When we were alone, they would often explain why they acted in certain situations the way they did, what they felt to be the burdens of their authority, what the major problems doing surgery in a major medical center were, what the personal strengths and weaknesses of their colleagues were, and so on.

In addition, attendings used me often as a "clown" to diffuse tensions in the group. When things were going poorly, attendings on occasion would question me like any other member of the group and then poke fun at my fumbling and ignorance. Sitting around the doctors' lounge, the rigors of academic life would be compared unfavorably with those of surgery; and my manly virtues would be impugned. It was not always as a clown that attendings used me to ease tensions. Just as with housestaff, I was asked to referee conflict. My study was used by them to deflect conversations from their course. So that often when faced with troublesome questions from nurses or other physicians, they would give a noncommittal response and then ask me to explain my study. They would ply me with questions until they were sure the conversation could safely resume.

*   *   *

The problem of objective description and analysis is in itself formidable. In fieldwork, the problem is made more complex because of the deep relationships and attachments one builds over time to one's subjects. As Charles Lidz[1] has correctly pointed out, the right and privilege of being an observer is a gift presented to the researcher by his host and subjects. I would agree with Lidz that the recognition and proper understanding of the gift relationship serves as both a convenient theoretical framework for understanding the peculiar dilemmas of the fieldworker and at the same time a formidable restraint on bias in observation and interpretation.

The giver and the recipient of a gift are involved in an interactional sequence that involves giving, receiving, and reciprocating. Even more important, involvement in a gift cycle creates a solidarity among participants and signifies that they have obligations toward each other that extend into the future. The fact that the fieldworker is both the receiver of a gift and a guest means that he has a diffuse sense of obligation to his host-giver-subject. Fieldworkers have long recognized their indebtedness to their subjects. While not explicitly analyzing the observer role as a gift relationship, fieldworkers worry over fulfilling their obligations to their subjects, over balancing personal debts to individuals against universal debts to the discipline of sociology, and over discharging obligations to subjects that extend beyond the life of any particular piece of research. In addition, there is the fieldworker's typical ethical dilemma: What if the data I gather are potentially harmful to my subjects? What if the facts themselves betray those to whom I have become so attached over so many months? Others have spoken of the "tyranny of the gift" in different contexts, but it is clear that the gift of access, of witnessing social life as it is lived in someone else's environment, exercises a tyranny of its own. This tyranny has as its most distinctive features three significant elements: (1)

the danger of overrapport, so thoroughly merging with the subject's point of view that one cannot achieve the critical distance necessary for analysis; (2) the danger of overindebtedness, so thoroughly feeling a sense of diffuse obligation that one can no longer assess what one does and does not properly owe his subjects; and (3) the danger of overgeneralization, so thoroughly idealizing one's subjects that one sees their behavior as overly representative of all persons in a class.

I was protected from overrapport and overindebtedness in part by the very structure of hospital life. Unlike fieldworkers who spend years with an unchanging population, my subjects rotated through the surgical services fairly rapidly. Some stayed for as little as a month; none stayed over three months. There were housestaff I liked very much; housestaff I detested; and others I barely got to know. Whatever the case, there was an unending parade of housestaff. The mere fact that I was observing so many people in rapid succession prevented overrapport with any one subject.

My resolution to the problem of overindebtedness was somewhat different from the resolution of the problem of overrapport. A moderately sensitive observer of life in the surgery wards of a hospital will be flooded with feelings of helplessness. These feelings themselves have two distinct components. First, witnessing so much pain and suffering, the fieldworker wants to roll up his sleeves and do something, anything. At the same time, seeing death as an everyday event makes one guilty and overly aware of one's own good fortune. As a fieldworker, I was often made uncomfortable by what I saw. I felt I had stumbled into incredibly intimate and significant slices of patients' and doctors' lives. Much like any person who sees more than he would like of a friend's life, I felt guilty about some of the knowledge I had gained, worried over what the boundary between privileged information and data was, and wondered about how I repaid my obligation to my subjects. In the short run, the housestaff resolved the problem of helplessness and indebtedness by the roles they cast for me. When housestaff demanded that I help out by wheeling the chart rack, opening dressings, acting as a group memory, they provided me a means to cope with my own helplessness and assuage my guilt at the same time that they incorporated me into the group.

Overgeneralization is also a recurrent problem for fieldworkers. There is the danger that one particular event will become etched in the fieldworker's memory as emblematic of the way action is organized in an environment. That is to say, fieldworkers may overgeneralize incidents and see them as representative of categories of action. I avoided overgeneralization by making sure I had at least two independently generated examples of the same phenomenon before I began to make inferences. My operating rule here was, as far as I can see, not fundamentally different from those that survey researchers use to ensure reliability in their studies. Also, I was very careful to follow particular incidents through many levels of social organization. For example, I was able to test my inferences about normative error in the promotion meeting, where I observed the criteria attending surgeons use to judge the fitness of housestaff for surgical careers. Throughout my fieldwork, I was very careful to test observations in one context against those of another.

On the other hand, there are observations I made that did not find their way into the fieldwork because I felt my inferential base was too thin. On one occasion I watched a series of unexpected deaths and complications, which occurred in quick succession, temporarily destroy the morale of one of the services I was observing. These occurred during the end of a rotation, while a chief resident was on vacation. I developed an explanation which related the occurrence of failure and group panic. However, during the rest of my fieldwork, I did not have the opportunity to observe another rash of failures. As a result, such speculations did not find their way into my published work.

*   *   *

When I was in the middle of the field, disguising the place and principals of my study was not as easy as it is in this report. I was always aware when I spoke that others knew those I spoke of, and that a too-loose tongue could hurt me and them in many untold ways. Since I promised my subjects confidentiality and anonymity, the "cover story" I devised to manage social situations was as consequential as the one I devised to manage field introductions. Only by assuring confidentiality and anonymity could I satisfy my subjects that my study would be within the bounds of current medical ethics. Both promises present some dilemmas, however.

First, I could never be sure that some enterprising person would not be able to figure out my place and principals. Essentially, confidentiality and anonymity were the promises I made but I had little control over their fulfillment. There have been recent debates about whether fieldworkers should go to the bother of making general "covering names" for their sites, and whether they should disguise their subjects. It seems to me that such fictitious names do more than provide confidentiality and anonymity: They highlight the generalized features of our descriptions and minimize the particularized aspects. To my mind, this aspect of naming is even more important in some ways than confidentiality and anonymity in that it creates a fieldwork literature rather than a description of specific places.

Others have advocated that to make fieldwork more rigorous and to display our methodology more openly, we should open our notebooks to the curious. Such procedure would allow others to see how we manipulate our data and fit the canons of science in general. Such a proposal troubles me because, as a sociologist, I gathered litigable material from subjects who trusted me. As a sociologist, I have no legal right to claim a privileged or confidential relationship with my subjects; my notes are subpoenable. If I opened my notebooks in the manner necessary to make clear the operations I performed on my data, I risk having those notebooks put to uses other than those I approve of. Involved here is a difficult problem: how to afford my subjects and myself enough protection so that we feel comfortable doing the study, at the same time displaying my data in a way that assures others of the validity and reliability of my research. I have indicated what I have done to satisfy myself. For the moment, I suggest that this is the best I can do.

*　　*　　*

If it is correct to say that the primary task of the fieldworker is to experience the rhythms, shadings, and emotional tones of social life, then it is also permissible to ask: What difference does such an analysis make? This question has no simple answer. But perhaps we can provide a rough outline of two major dimensions of any adequate response to the question: "Why fieldwork?"

First, fieldwork puts us directly in touch with the human dimensions of social life in a way that no other method of inquiry does. This is true because fieldwork forces us first to experience those dimensions and then to find words to describe them. Full understanding involves an intimate contact and this is what fieldwork provides. It allows us to describe a set of fundamental life experiences as they occur. Fieldwork supplies precisely what other methods of research drop out—the experiencing individual as a member of a community and the set of shared meanings that sustains that individual's action in an uncertain world. Fieldwork allows us to see social life as we live it.

But that is not all that fieldwork provides. It supplies us with an opportunity not just to describe the lives that we lead but to analyze them. When it is performed with skill, it allows us to examine the fit between principles and practice. Fieldwork, then, provides a mirror for looking at who we are as against who we would like to be. It provides us with soft data—observations, intuitions, and comments—for rethinking some very hard questions about what it means to be a member of the society.

NOTE

1. Charles Lidz, "Rethinking Rapport: Problems of Reciprocal Obligations in Participant Observation Research." Paper presented at the annual meeting of the Eastern Sociological Association, New York, March 1977. See also Marcel Mauss, *The Gift* (New York: W. W. Norton, 1967).

The Outsider Phenomenon

NANCY A. NAPLES

In the early 1990s, while teaching at Iowa State University, Nancy Naples conducted an ethnographic study of two small towns in rural Iowa. The study was initially designed to explore how low-income women in rural communities were affected by the social and economic restructuring of their towns as a result of changes in the global economy and the accompanying decline of the welfare state. Naples hoped to compare urban and rural community activists, but found few women who were willing to speak out. After a local egg processing plant expanded and the numbers of Mexican and Mexican-American residents increased, she refocused the study to explore the restructuring of racial and ethnic relations as well as gender and class.

A secondary goal of Naples's research was to examine the adequacy of the insider/outsider distinction as a guideline for evaluating and conducting ethnographic research. In this selection she shows that, rather than taking a single "insider" or "outsider" perspective, social scientists who conduct ethnographic research relate to the residents of the communities they study along numerous dimensions. Moreover, "outsiderness" and "insiderness" are not fixed or static positions but ever-shifting and permeable social locations. Thus, when conducting ethnographic research in their country of origin, social scientists are simultaneously insiders and outsiders.

Portions of this selection are excerpted from "A Feminist Revisiting of the 'Outsider/Insider' Debate: The 'Outsider Phenomenon' in Rural Iowa," *Qualitative Sociology*, vol. 19, no. 1, 1996.

The purpose of this chapter is to demonstrate the value of a feminist perspective on community studies with particular attention to the debate contrasting insider and outsider ethnographic research.[1] The insider versus outsider debate—whether it is more effective to conduct fieldwork as an insider or an outsider to the communities you study—challenges those of us who use ethnographic methods in our research in the United States to reexamine our taken-for-granted assumptions about what constitutes "indigenous" knowledge and how we use both our commonalities and differences to heighten sensitivity to others' complex and shifting world views.

In this feminist revisiting of the insider/outsider debate, I argue that the insider/outsider distinction masks the power differentials and experiential differences between the researcher and the researched. The bipolar construction of insider/outsider also sets up a false separation that neglects the interactive processes through which "insiderness" and "outsiderness" are constructed. Insiderness and outsiderness are not fixed or static positions, rather they are ever-shifting and permeable social locations that are differentially experienced and expressed by community members. By recognizing the fluidity of insiderness/outsiderness, we also acknowledge three key methodological points: as ethnographers we are never fully outside or inside the community; our relationship to the community is never expressed in general terms but is constantly being negotiated and renegotiated in particular, everyday interactions; and these interactions are themselves located in shifting relationships among community residents. These negotiations simultaneously are embedded in processes that reposition gender, class, and racial–ethnic relations among other socially constructed distinctions. From a feminist perspective, I argue that by shifting the standpoint to those who are marginal to the mythic community insider, certain less visible features of community life are brought into view.

The apparently clear distinction between insiderness and outsiderness falls away as we confront how regional differences, as well as class, gender, age, parenting and marital status, sexuality, race, and ethnicity shape the multiple identities we identify (with) in our research. I start with the assumption that, rather than one insider perspective, we all begin our work from different positions and social experiences that contribute to numerous dimensions on which we can relate to residents in various overlapping communities. Our social location shapes the way we enter the field and how we relate to different members within a particular community. For example, as a woman I have certain experiences that may give me greater insider perspectives on women I meet in the field. However, my research with African-American and Puerto Rican women in low income communities in New York City and Philadelphia underscored for me the diverse ways that women's experiences are shaped by race, class, sex, and religious commitment, among other dimensions. On the other hand, as a New York City native and a social worker in Manhattan I was familiar with many more features of social life when conducting this urban-centered research than I was in my research in rural Iowa.

Before I continue, it is necessary to situate myself within my own social cultural background. I was born into a working class family and lived until August of 1989 in New York City. I spent eight years as a social worker, community resident, and political activist in Manhattan. My dissertation involved research in the South Bronx, Harlem, and the Lower East Side of Manhattan, and with low income communities in Philadelphia. Following the completion of my Ph.D. and much to the amazement of many of my friends, I accepted a faculty position at Iowa State University. The shift from the large urban sprawl of New York City to the small town and largely rural surroundings of Ames, Iowa, inspired a vast array of empirical and theoretical questions that have permanently altered the way I view the world.

When I arrived in Iowa, I was intrigued by the contrast between rural and urban community life. What began as a modest attempt to compare the experiences of low income women in rural Iowa with the urban women I had studied in New York City and Philadelphia has now developed into an extensive and ongoing ethnographic study of the changing gender, class, and racial–ethnic relations in two small towns with populations of under 1,500 residents. With the assistance of a grant from the National Institute of Mental Health, I began an ethnographic study of the social dimensions of rural economic and demographic change. Since so much of my worldview has been shaped within an urban context, I felt very much the outsider when I entered a rural setting. Despite the surface commonality of language, I was completely ignorant of a rural way of life. Ironically, many of those I met in Iowa were baffled by those of us from large urban settings. At the close of a 1991 interview with a farmer, she asked about my background and when I told her she said: "How can you stand having all those people around?" I then described my discomfort with the lack of people in the open spaces of Iowa.

One theme pervading the data gathered in the field is the extent to which residents with a diversity of social, economic, and demographic characteristics experienced feelings of alienation from the perceived community at large. In fact, most people I interviewed in-depth said they were outsiders to the community for a variety of differing reasons. My own feelings of outsiderness became a resource through which I was able to acquire an insider perspective on many residents' perception of alienation from others in their community.

This finding appears to support Georg Simmel's contention that people will share confidences with a stranger that they may not share with friends and acquaintances.[2] Yet the parallel finding that many residents also felt themselves outside the community led me to reexamine the insider/outsider debate and to identify what I have come to call the "outsider phenomenon." Simmel's analysis was based on a rigid conception of social life that assumed an unchanging distinction between the stranger and the insider; an inattention to power in encounters between the stranger and insiders; and a belief in the stranger's greater objectivity. In this feminist revisiting, I highlight the fluidity of outsiderness and insiderness; center attention on power in ethnographic encounters; and challenge reductive and essentialist notions of standpoint. Rather than view insiderness/outsiderness as identifiable and relatively fixed social locations, the concept of outsider phenomenon highlights the processes through which community members are created as others—a process in which all members participate to varying degrees—and by which feelings of otherness are incorporated into self-perceptions and social interactions. The identification of the outsider phenomenon is especially noteworthy given the continued salience of gemeinschaft found in accounts of rural small town life offered by residents and nonresidents alike.

The often used distinction between *gemeinschaft* and *geselleschaft* serves to mask differences in small communities as well as underestimate the close-knit experiences of community in urban areas. The one obvious difference confronted in rural-based research is the obvious paucity of public places/spaces for entry into the field. The lack of public spaces is a disadvantage to an outsider; however, I found access to personal spaces in rural communities easier than in urban settings. As my research progressed, I became more convinced than ever that place profoundly influences the way we see the world around us. Therefore, women of the same class or race background may be unable to bridge the different worldviews shaped by geographic variations in their experiences. On the other hand, as the research progressed, I was surprised to learn that many residents in these two rural towns also felt like outsiders, albeit for different reasons. The mutual outsider feelings became a deeply felt and widely expressed basis for the fieldwork and subsequent analysis. Ironically, my outsider status served as a means by which I became an insider to the outsider feelings of many interviewed for the study. Simultaneously, my insider designation as a faculty member at Iowa State, a popular state university, provided an initial ground for residents' willingness to share their experiences with me.

I interviewed a subset of community members, including clergy, social service workers, and low income women, on two or more occasions. Interviews took place in offices, in homes, at local restaurants, less formally on Main Street, in local businesses during working hours, or while attending community events. The open-ended interview was utilized to generate an oral history of each community resident with special attention to the following areas: background; education and work experiences; attitudes toward his or her community; economic development; gender, race–ethnic, and class relations; participation in community activities; and a description of changes in the town and visions for the future.

One strategy I used to gain a broader understanding of the social construction of community included gathering in-depth information from diverse perspectives—a commonplace fieldwork method. I also utilized group discussions with selected community members to further explore some of the themes identified in the interviews. In these small group discussions, I posed specific questions about the community that were generated from my interviews and other data gathering efforts. Responses from the group helped clarify my findings (or hunches) and, in some instances, redirected my investigations. These discussions often occurred in the course of other activities and sometimes included residents of nearby communities as well as Midtown and Southtown (the pseudonyms for the two towns in this study). These often impromptu discussions were enriched by the presence of nonresidents as they helped further highlight the differences between nonindigenous but contiguous perspectives and indigenous constructions. However, rarely did any one group include a variety of perspectives from within the two towns. Mexicans and Mexican Americans (who had moved to Midtown for employment in an expanding food processing plant located on the outskirts of the town) rarely met informally with non-Spanish-speaking white residents. Low income residents rarely spoke openly about their perceptions and experiences in a group discussion with those they perceived as more economically secure.

As mentioned, a majority of the community residents interviewed reported feelings of alienation from the perceived wider community. Ironically, those who were defined by others as insiders, also said they felt like outsiders who will never be accepted. I often left Midtown and Southtown after a field trip asking: "Who are the insiders here?" I have yet to meet a community resident who feels completely like the mythical community insider. Those named as insiders, such as the owners of the food processing plant and the local bankers, also feel like outsiders as they perceive other community residents' resentment of their economic success and political clout. Erin Landers (a pseudonym), one of the plant owners and a longtime resident of Midtown, reported that she felt a number of community members, particularly older residents who knew her and her husband as children, resented their financial success. She also perceived hostility from community members who were displeased with the number of Mexican and Mexican Americans who had moved to Midtown for employment in the plant.

Embedded in the outsider phenomenon were the patterns of inequality that shaped social life in these two rural towns. While those with more political and economic resources also felt outside for reasons often associated with their power and wealth, those with less resources were more disadvantaged by the social control processes associated with the outsider phenomenon. The mythic construction of a gemeinschaft-like community fed into the outsider phenomenon. The idealized construction of what it meant to be a part of the community and of who were legitimate community members served as both an internalized and externalized means of social control. When someone spoke up to challenge the construction, they were formally silenced or ostracized. Others silenced themselves for fear that they would disrupt the fragile sense of community. Consequently, many members walked around feeling alienated from the mythic community yet were careful not to share their feelings with others who they perceived were more connected to the community. As long as those on the margins felt silenced by the outsider phenomenon they would not challenge the power base and definition of the situation that privileged a small elite who controlled town politics and economic development.

On the other hand, a number of events and shifts in definition we chronicled highlighted the fluidity of the outsider phenomenon. This is most evident when we examine the process of racialization[3] in Midtown. Mexicans and Mexican Americans were most likely to fit into the taken-for-granted definition of newcomer (one important dimension of outsiderness) as they were among the most recent arrivals in Midtown. However, the term *newcomer* was also used to differentiate between "Americans" and others viewed as temporary and, oftentimes, illegitimate residents. Under this formulation, Mexican Americans were frequently categorized along with undocumented Mexican workers as illegal and posing numerous problems for the so-called legitimate members of the community. However, the process of racialization in Midtown demonstrates that such totalizing conceptualization of the Mexican and Mexican-American residents was unstable and, consequently, quickly fell apart in the face of interactions with different agents of the state, such as the police and agents of the Immigration and Naturalization Service. The totalization was further compromised as young Mexican and Mexican Americans entered the school system, were adopted by local families, dated white European-American teenagers or married local white residents.

The documented shift in construction of outsiderness with regard to the Mexican and Mexican-American residents highlights the fluidity of standpoints when viewed over time. Yet the tensions between white European-American and Mexican and Mexican-American residents remain. As my field investigations focused increasingly on the experiences of the Mexican and Mexican-American residents and the process of racialization in Midtown, I was also repositioned by formerly receptive informants, especially those who held positions of power in the town. This repositioning was furthered when I hired bilingual Chicano graduate student Lionel Cantú to assist with the project. Where I found no difficulty moving freely about the town, Mr. Cantú reported being followed by the police, having his mail tampered with, and fearing for his safety.

On the other hand, Mr. Cantú quickly won the trust of many Mexican and Mexican-American residents, a trust that would be difficult for me to gain as an Anglo non-Spanish-speaking researcher. In fact, when Anna Ortega (a pseudonym) was concerned with increasing police harassment in the town, she phoned Mr. Cantú in California for assistance. After some deliberation, we decided to mobilize my network of contacts in Iowa who were working as advocates for Latino residents in other parts of the state. My hesitation in connecting her with these advocates related to fear of exposing her position as an informal recruiter of numerous Mexican and Mexican-American workers and their families. When Mr. Cantú returned her call and asked if we could give her name to several people who we thought might be able to assist her in dealing with the town officials, she agreed. In her role as recruiter and as a Latina, she felt more responsible for the well-being of those she brought to Midtown than was evidenced by the plant owners who, we suspect, initially sponsored her activities.

Our incorporation into the racialization process in Midtown and our dilemma over how to negotiate a more activist involvement in the community formed but two key tensions we confronted. The racialization process was illustrative of the ways in which the ethnographic field shifted over time and limited our ability to make one unchanging position on any methodological dilemma we faced.

THE PERSONAL POLITICS OF FIELDWORK

I listened with great empathy to the feelings of alienation expressed throughout the ethnographic interviews. One woman asked that I turn the tape recorder off while she composed herself after sharing her sadness over what she saw as the futile attempts of the economic development committee to revitalize the economy of her small town. Yet she had little hope that any other strategies would improve the economic well-being of her neighbors and friends. I also witnessed numerous processes of exclusion that formed the basis of many social exchanges between low income residents, especially single mothers, and more middle class residents. The white European-American residents' treatment of the Mexican and Mexican-American residents in Midtown was, at times, particularly discriminatory and difficult to witness. Although I harbor no inherent animosity toward the elite of these small towns, I have less empathy with their expressions of outsiderness as I witness their power to define the lives of others. I do admit a certain bias in my empathy toward those on the margins of these small towns that most likely reflect my own feelings of marginalization in many social locations. Yet as a sociologist, I am constantly aware that individual actions are embedded in the wider social cultural and economic processes. For example, I can take the point of view of the owner of a food processing plant who firmly believes that the minimum wage jobs are fair and that all workers are treated equally. However, this plant owner does not find it necessary to take the point of view of the workers in the plant who have different standpoints on the pay and organization of the workplace. From her privileged position, she can deny the power inherent in her ability to ignore the perspectives of those she employs.

How to locate myself in relationship to different community residents continues to haunt me in ongoing as well as sporadic ethnographic encounters. I found a partial solution in Patricia Hill Collins's analysis of the "ethic of caring" in Black feminist thought.[4] She describes the ethic of caring with reference to three interrelated dimensions: an "emphasis on individual uniqueness," "the appropriateness of emotions in dialogues," and "the capacity for empathy." As I gathered data in Midtown and Southtown and identified the outsider phenomenon, I further explored the notion of outsiderness to get underneath residents' public presentations of self. I shared my own feelings to a certain extent and explored the similarities and differences between my experiences and those of the community residents interviewed. I utilized multiple opportunities to dialogue with diverse community members, drawing on my own feelings of outsiderness and enhancing my capacity for empathy in each of these encounters.

Traditional guidelines for ethnographic research include: gaining entry, building relationships, preserving objectivity, and maintaining the observer's role. In my own work, I find that gaining entry and building relationships automatically interfere with the third guideline, preserving objectivity (if such a stance were possible at all). As mentioned, one strategy I used to gain a broader understanding of the social construction of community included gathering in-depth information from diverse perspectives. I also took advantage of group discussions with community members to help set the agenda and reflect on the research process. Yet I do not grant all members of the community equal roles in helping me reflect on the research. Certain community members would obviously not be sympathetic to my explicitly feminist, anti-racist, and social democratic perspective. I was also careful in sharing my lesbian identity with people in this small town. In fact, the social control processes clearly affected my choice in sharing certain features of my own life with those I interacted with in Midtown and Southtown. As a consequence of my experience of the outsider phenomenon, I relied more heavily on conversations and group discussions with more progressive elements within the community than with others in the two towns.

The second guideline, building relationships, is a direct consequence of the first and raises a basic moral or ethical dilemma for the field-worker. Most guides to ethnographic research recognize this dilemma but conclude that the benefits of increasing our knowledge about different groups in our social world far outweighs the drawbacks. However, the dilemma continues to surface in our daily encounters in the field. The apparently straightforward question, What is data?, is often one of the most difficult questions to answer. At times, I clearly understood what was possible and ethical to observe and record. At other times, I had a feeling that to record particular observations or statements would be an invasion of the participants' privacy. There were times I recognized that the re-searcher role violated the trust gained in the course of the fieldwork. These moments increased as the personal encounters increased. As Susan Stern described in her participatory research project with parents in a public school district outside Washington, D.C., she was often confused about whether a particular encounter with a community resident was data or friendship.[5] The longer she lives in the community, the less data she can accumulate about the community women who are now her friends. On the other hand, Stern argues that friendship is an underexplored basis and rich arena for generating indigenous knowledge. I have contin-ued friendships with two women whom I met through the fieldwork. Each provides me with knowledgeable feedback on the preliminary findings of the research. They constantly challenge my presuppositions and help me clarify terms so that I might remain true to the complex social processes that contribute to the vitality of rural life. I have grown reliant on their wise counsel as I continue to make sense of the social construction of community in rural Iowa.

Building relationships is, of course, a necessary part of gaining trust and access in ethnographic encounters. Less acknowledged in much of the fieldwork literature are the emotional consequences for the re-searcher when, over the course of fieldwork, more distanced relationships are transformed into friendships. Emotions are always present in personal interactions in ethnographic work. Here the feminist perspective is useful in reminding us that emotions can form an important basis for under-standing and analysis. Because a primary goal of feminist research is to uncover how inequality is reproduced and resisted, how we draw on our capacity for empathy and emotion is directly related to a deep commit-ment to this political project. The use of dialogue as well as emotion and empathy were especially valuable tools for clarifying the tensions between individual narratives and identification of broader processes like racializa-tion and the outsider phenomenon that are hidden from an individual resident's direct sight.

The third guideline, preserving objectivity, is especially troubling for feminist researchers. However, the research process always invites questions of power and control. No matter what kinds of participatory processes we employ in our work, the researcher still retains control over the decisions regarding who benefits from the research, who controls the dissemination of the findings, and who determines the particular processes chosen for the research. The more self-reflective we are about the social structure of research and our own position within that structure, the less we will fall prey to the false belief that we can be objective in our search.

The outsider phenomenon and my methodological reflections on the interaction between my own outsider feelings and those of community members highlights the value of a feminist standpoint methodology for challenging the false divide between insider/outsider research and between so-called objective or scientific and indigenous knowledge. The insights of feminist theories are helpful in examining the differences between ethnographic research in a variety of settings. We start with our position vis-à-vis the community and various community members to determine the personal tensions we confront as we enter different terrains. A consistent theme in feminist approaches includes an emphasis on self-awareness and self-reflection. We need to understand our own cultural biases and assumptions in order to examine the ways they influence the research process and analysis. Our gender, race–ethnicity, class, sexual orientation, age, political perspectives, as well as regional and cultural backgrounds provide a rich canvas on which to evaluate differences and similarities in the field.

Furthermore, this feminist revisiting of the insider/outsider debate demonstrates the limits of Georg Simmel's and other standpoint analyses that neglect the interaction between shifting power relations in a community context. As newcomers to these rural towns, I and my research assistants are implicated in these processes and inevitably become a party to the renegotiations as we interact with different community members whose positions are shifting over time. Identification of the outsider phenomenon and my methodological reflections on the interactions between my own outsider feelings and those of community members highlighted for me how processes of inequality and resistance shaped social life in these small towns. In particular, the process of racialization documented in the course of the fieldwork demonstrated how insider/outsider positions were ever-shifting and permeable social locations. On the other hand, standpoints within the outsider phenomenon are informed by material processes that organize class divisions and gender and racial inequality, among other dimensions. By highlighting processes through which outsiderness was constructed and reconstituted, this feminist analysis reveals how as ethnographers we are never fully outside or inside the community.

I expect to continue this exploration of the outsider phenomenon as I delve deeper into the social construction of community and resistance in rural Iowa. I hope to remain self-conscious of my own assumptions as they influence my relationships with residents in these communities and shape my analysis of the ethnographic data. I can never fully enter into the worldview of those whose lives are shaped by a rural cultural experience nor will I ever fully know the experiences of women from the small towns I study. Yet, keeping aware of the differences I perceive as well as the similarities I discover will help bridge the gap to a certain extent. Acknowledging the tension and shifts between feelings of outsiderness and insiderness for myself as well as for the community residents will help make salient these contrasts. To a certain extent, we all suffer from the outsider phenomenon; yet we can also benefit from it as we recognize how we share this experience with so many others.

NOTES

1. See especially Dorothy E. Smith, *The Everyday World as Problematic: Towards a Feminist Sociology* (Toronto: University of Toronto Press, 1987).

2. Georg Simmel, "The Sociological Significance of the 'Stranger.' " In R. E. Park and E. W. Burgess, eds., *Introduction to the Science of Sociology* (Chicago: University of Chicago Press, 1921).

3. Howard Winant, *Racial Conditions* (Minneapolis: University of Minnesota Press, 1994).

4. Patricia Hill Collins, *Black Feminist Thought* (Boston: Unwin Hyman, 1990).

5. Susan Stern, *Social Science from Below: Grassroots Knowledge for Science and Emancipation.* Unpublished dissertation, City University of New York, 1994.

Epilogue

Finding Your Spot

VERNON BOGGS

In a famous account of the process of getting into the field, Carlos Castaneda describes how Don Juan, the Yaqui Indian medicine man whom he sought as a mentor, refused to sponsor him until he had solved a riddle. He must find the spot (sitio) on the porch of the Indian's house where he could feel happy and strong. Not every place was good to sit or be on, the medicine man explained. Within the confines of the porch there was one spot that was unique, where the ethnographer could be at his very best. After a grueling night spent trying out first one and then another spot on the hard porch floor, Castaneda fell asleep in frustration. When he awoke, refreshed after a heavy sleep, the medicine man greeted him: "You have found the spot," he said.

Castaneda's metaphor describes the frustration and uncertainty all ethnographers experience as they seek to find the places and people with whom they will feel comfortable in developing their research. In this epilogue Vernon Boggs describes how he discovered that places that have had great meaning to him could become the "spots" for his research. He shows how he used the Afro-Hispanic dimension of his early experiences to formulate an ethnographic research project about black and latin cultural synthesis. As is true of many ethnographers, Boggs's motivations were at first highly subjective; he wished to gain a better understanding of some aspects of his own experience and upbringing. As a professional social scientist, however, Boggs also realized that his experiences afforded him certain insights into an important area of changing race and cultural relations.

Too often, he believed, jazz and blues have been interpreted as a unique cultural expression of the experience of African Americans in North America. This view essentially ignores a powerful, ever-changing cultural idiom, rendering it a subject of history rather than a field for ethnographic exploration. Throughout much of Latin America, the Caribbean, and Africa, as well as in the cosmopolitan centers of the Western nations, jazz and local rhythms are being fused into new forms of popular music such as soucusse, pachanga, hi-life, and reggae. Boggs's work is part of a growing trend in the study of culture that traces the spread and synthesis of world cultures, in this case the African and Hispanic influences on New World music.

Boggs wrote a number of articles on clave, the fundamental rhythm of Latin American musical traditions. He was deeply engaged in research on the origins of this cultural synthesis and the social institutions that sustain its growth. His book, Salsiology, *is likely to become a classic in the emerging field of cultural studies.*

When I was about 10 years old, my aunt asked me what I wanted for my upcoming birthday. I told her that I wanted a record called "Anabacoa." She promised to buy it if I could spell the name. I do not remember if I spelled it correctly or not, but I did get the record. Now, as I reflect on that early experience, I wonder how it was that such a record interested me so. I could not speak Spanish then. At home we heard only gospel music, and I have no idea why I was attracted to the latin sound. In any case, these early influences led me to wonder a great deal about my early experiences outside my own culture.

Another strong childhood memory is that of the cowboy movie. I began going to the movies alone at about 12 years of age. I particularly loved the Dracula-meets-Wolfman and Frankenstein flicks. Popeye was also a hero. But the cowboy films captured most of my attention. I identified with the Mexicans in those films. I began to dream of learning Spanish, and when I began high school, Spanish was my first elective course. I showed ability in language and was rewarded for my efforts, but I was also shy and doubted my linguistic abilities.

While in high school I hung out a great deal on the streets of Atlantic City, New Jersey, my hometown. This was during the 1950s, and "doo-wop," the early a capella form of rock and roll, reigned supreme. Sam Cook had recorded "My Baby Loves to Cha Cha Cha," and Ruth Brown had made a hit with "Mambo Baby." Again my attraction to the latin beat in black music took over, and while my friends and I stood outside the clubs on Kentucky Avenue, especially Club Harlem and Gracie's Little Belmont, I found myself impassioned by any jazz that included that latin beat. However, none of us had money to buy records, and the latin sound was especially hard to locate.

Then I heard the great Nat King Cole's recordings in Spanish, and I knew I had to have them. Here was a non-Hispanic singing beautiful melodies in Spanish. Somehow I managed to buy a copy. I played it over and over until I knew all the lyrics by heart. Then—still in the early 1950s—I heard about a club in New York City called the Palladium. I made up my mind to visit it and began saving my money from caddying at the local golf courses for a trip to New York.

One Friday evening in 1955 I took the bus to New York City. When I arrived, I took the subway to Harlem, a section of the city I knew nothing about. I found a cheap hotel room, and within a couple of hours I was at the Palladium Ballroom on 53rd and Broadway. Although technically I was too young to enter the club, I was allowed in. I still remember how the lighting and the music "blew me away." I felt that I was really and truly home. I had been looking for this music for years and this was it. I went back to New Jersey determined to spend as much time as I could at the Palladium.

In 1956 I joined the U.S. Naval Reserves, and in 1957 I was sent on active duty and assigned to the *U.S.S. Albemarle.* In 1958, as luck would have it, we were sent to Guantanamo, Cuba. I was in the heartland of clave, or Afro-Hispanic music, although I didn't know it at the time. From there we sailed to Montego Bay and Port of Spain, where I got a taste of reggae and calypso. Our next port of call was San Juan, Puerto Rico, the home of bomba and plena, two branches of clave.

I fell in love with San Juan. I went to a restaurant, found a jukebox, and played a record whose lyrics I did not fully understand and even today cause me some consternation. It was a song about a Negro who doesn't leave home because he's so ugly that whenever he does, the women who see him in the street faint. I probed the city for more Afro-Hispanic music. Curiously enough, I and some other servicemen found our way to a hot hangout in San Juan called the Palladium. What interested me about the place was that the same music was being played that I had heard in the States, except that it was not live. By the time my ship left San Juan, I had become a devotee of Afro-Hispanic music. I knew very little about its origins or rhythmic patterns—clave—but I loved it.

During the 1960s I began hanging out at the Palladium and Birdland in New York. My social life revolved around music: I went to dances at the St. George Hotel, Riverside Plaza, Hunt's Point Plaza, and other places too numerous to mention. I listened to Symphony Sid's nightly show and to Ricardo "Dick" Sugar. When Sid retired, I listened to his replacement, Joe Gaines. The Palladium folded in the mid-1960s, but aficionados of Afro-Hispanic music jammed the Cheetah on 52nd Street and 8th Avenue and the Village Gate, with its weekly Monday night series, "Salsa Meets Jazz," hosted by Symphony Sid. The music itself began to change from the mambo/cha cha craze to the latin boogaloo/charanga mode. However, in 1969 I began visiting Europe and within five years had moved there and become involved in research on other subjects. Music was on the back burner.

In the late 1970s I was a sociologist interested in urban ecology, deviance, and crime, but I did not realize that my love of Afro-Hispanic music could lead to professional research. But then I discovered that a colleague was teaching a course in the sociology of music. I suggested that he add a lecture on latin music, and he responded that his knowledge in this area was too limited and asked that I present the lecture. Although I accepted his offer, I realized that my knowledge of the subject was superficial in that everything I knew about the music had come from listening to it. If I was to address an audience on this subject, I would have to approach it more systematically.

I prepared my lecture on "Salsa Music" by reviewing my tapes of on-the-air discussions and conducting a review of the literature in various libraries and archives. I later edited the lecture and submitted it for publication in *Popular Music and Society*. Although these efforts were successful as far as they went, I realized that there was a great deal that was missing from my knowledge of the origins and spread of these musical forms. And so I began a more extensive research project.

Although the music I have been referring to is commonly called latin jazz, salsa, Afro-Cuban jazz, and other names, it is a genre that can most accurately be termed Afro-Hispanic because its roots are partly in Africa and partly in Europe and it is characteristic of Spanish-speaking societies in the Western Hemisphere. These facts were unknown to me for several decades. In addition to the racial component of the music, I also learned about its class component in the countries where it was "born." It had never occurred to me that before the 1970s this was considered lower-class black music in Afro-Hispanic societies. Even Cubans and Puerto Ricans classified it as such. Furthermore, I learned that Afro-Cuban musicians like Mario Bauza and Frank "Grillo" Machito had forged early alliances with African-American jazz musicians like Dizzy Gillespie and Charlie Parker in order to broaden the appeal of their music. And that while middle- and upper-class fair-skinned Cubans, Puerto Ricans, and other Hispanics shunned the music, middle- and upper-class fair-skinned American Jews and other American white ethnic groups supported and promoted it.

I had also noted in my travels that many white Europeans were fans of Afro-Hispanic music, just as they are collectors and fans of jazz. But this does not imply that clave is in danger of becoming only an art form (a problem faced by classical jazz in North America). Throughout much of Latin America and Brazil, the Caribbean and Africa, and many large American cities, clave is a living cultural form with new dances and new variations emerging all the time. In fact, clave is a worldwide cultural complex.

A fortunate set of circumstances led me to realize that my lifelong love of music and language could also be a subject of professional research. Now I am deeply engaged in conducting interviews with the creators of Afro-Hispanic music. These valuable life histories are only part of my study, though. I have also found my spot in New York once again, this time among the radio personalities who keep the music alive in this city and help promote it throughout North America. From there my research will branch out to all locations where Afro-Hispanic music is performed and created anew. *¡Que viva la musica!*

Selected Bibliography

Anderson, Elijah. *Streetwise: Race, Class, and Change in an Urban Community*. Chicago: University of Chicago Press, 1990.

———. *A Place on the Corner*. Chicago: University of Chicago Press, 1978, 1988.

Bandolier, Adolph. *The Delight Makers*. Orlando, Fla.: Harcourt Brace, 1973/1891.

Becker, Howard. *The Outsiders: Studies in the Sociology of Deviance*. New York: Free Press, 1963.

Bernard, H. Russell. *Research Methods in Cultural Anthropology*. Newbury Park, Calif.: Sage Publications, 1988.

Boggs, Vernon W. *Salsiology: Afro-Cuban Music and the Evolution of Salsa in New York City*. New York: Excelsior, 1992.

———. "Salsa Music: The Latent Function of Slavery and Racialism." *Journal of Popular Music and Society* 11, no. 1 (Spring 1987): 7–14.

Boggs, Vernon W., and Rolf Meyersohn. "The Profile of a Bronx Salsero: Salsa's Still Alive!" *Journal of Popular Music and Society* 12, no. 4 (Winter 1988): 59–67.

Boggs, Vernon W., Sylvia Fava, and Gerald Handel, eds. *The Apple Sliced: Sociological Studies of New York City*. South Hadley, Mass.: Bergin & Garvey, 1984.

Bosk, Charles. "The Fieldworker as Watcher and Witness." *Hastings Center Report* 15, no. 3 (June 1985): 10–14.

———. *Forgive and Remember: Managing Medical Failure*. Chicago: University of Chicago Press, 1979.

Bradburn, Norman M., Seymour Sudman, and Associates. *Improving Interview Method and Questionnaire Design*. San Francisco: Jossey-Bass, 1981.

Burawoy, Michael. *Ethnography Unbound: Power and Resistance in the Modern Metropolis*. Berkeley: University of California Press, 1991.

Castaneda, Carlos. *The Teachings of Don Juan: A Yaqui Way of Knowledge*. New York: Simon & Schuster, 1973.

Clifford, James, and George F. Marcus, eds. *Writing Culture: The Poetics and Politics of Ethnography.* Berkeley: University of California Press, 1986.

Epstein, Cynthia Fuchs. *Women in Law.* New York: Basic Books, 1981.

Erikson, Kai T. *A New Species of Trouble.* New York: Norton, 1994.

———. *Everything in Its Path: Destruction of Community in the Buffalo Creek Flood.* New York: Simon & Schuster, 1976.

Filstead, William J., ed. *Qualitative Methodology: Firsthand Involvement with the Social World.* Chicago: Markham, 1970.

Geertz, Clifford. *Interpretation of Cultures.* New York: Basic Books, 1973.

———. *Peddlers and Princes: Social Development and Economic Change in Two Indonesian Towns.* Chicago: University of Chicago Press, 1968.

Goffman, Erving. *Behavior in Public Places: Notes on the Social Organization of Gatherings.* New York: Free Press, 1966.

———. *Stigma: Notes on the Management of Spoiled Identity.* Englewood Cliffs, N.J.: Prentice-Hall, 1963.

———. *Presentation of Self in Everyday Life.* Garden City, N.Y.: Doubleday/Anchor, 1959.

Griffin, John Howard. *Black Like Me.* Boston: Houghton Mifflin, 1960.

Halsell, Grace. *Soul Sister.* New York: World, 1969.

Hammond, Philip E., ed. *Sociologists at Work.* New York: Basic Books, 1964.

Harper, Douglas. *Working Knowledge: Skill and Community in a Small Shop.* Chicago: University of Chicago Press, 1987.

———. *Good Company.* Chicago: University of Chicago Press, 1982.

Horowitz, Ruth. "Remaining an Outsider: Membership as a Threat to Research Rapport." *Urban Life* 14, no. 4 (January 1986): 409–430.

———. *Honor and the American Dream: Culture and Identity in a Chicago Neighborhood.* New Brunswick, N.J.: Rutgers University Press, 1985.

Hughes, Everett. *The Sociological Eye: Selected Papers.* New Brunswick, N.J.: Transaction, 1984.

Humphreys, Laud. *Tearoom Trade: Impersonal Sex in Public Places.* Hawthorne, N.Y.: Aldine de Gruyter, 1970, 1975.

Jacobs, Glenn, ed. *The Participant Observer: Encounters with Social Reality.* New York: George Braziller, 1970.

Kesey, Ken. *One Flew Over the Cuckoo's Nest.* New York: New American Library, 1962.

Kim, Illsoo. *New Urban Immigrants: The Korean Community in New York.* Princeton, N.J.: Princeton University Press, 1981.

Kornblum, William. "Working the Deuce." *Yale Review* (Spring 1988): 355–367.

———. "Boyash Gypsies: Shantytown Ethnicity." In Farnham Rehfisch, ed., *Gypsies, Tinkers and Other Travellers.* New York: Academic Press, 1975.

———. *Blue Collar Community.* Chicago: University of Chicago Press, 1974.

Liebow, Elliot. *Tally's Corner: A Study of Negro Streetcorner Men.* Boston: Little, Brown, 1967.

Lofland, John. *Analyzing Social Settings: A Guide to Qualitative Observation and Analysis,* 2nd ed. Belmont, Calif.: Wadsworth, 1984.

McNamara, Robert P. *The Times Square Hustler: Male Prostitution in New York City.* Westport, Conn.: Praeger, 1994.

Millman, Marcia. *The Unkindest Cut: Life in the Backrooms of Medicine.* New York: William Morrow, 1977.

Morales, Edmundo. *The Guinea Pig: Healing, Food, and Ritual in the Andes.* Tucson: University of Arizona Press, 1995.

————. *Cocaine: White Gold Rush in Peru.* Tucson: University of Arizona Press, 1989.

Myerhoff, Barbara. *Number Our Days.* New York: Simon & Schuster, 1978.

Nelson, William Javier. "Their Loss—Our Gain: The Gift of Latin Music to the U.S." *Afro-Hispanic Review* 6, no. 2 (May 1987): 19–24.

Schrank, Robert. *Ten Thousand Working Days.* Cambridge, Mass.: M.I.T. Press, 1978.

Stack, Carol. *All Our Kin.* New York: Harper & Row, 1974.

Wax, Rosalie. *Doing Fieldwork: Warnings and Advice.* Chicago: University of Chicago Press, 1971.

Whyte, William F. *Learning from the Field: A Guide from Experience.* Newbury Park, Calif.: Sage Publications, 1984.

————. *Street Corner Society: The Social Structure of an Italian Slum.* Chicago: University of Chicago Press, 1943.

Williams, Terry. *Crackhouse: Notes from the End of the Line.* Reading, Mass.: Addison-Wesley, 1992.

————. *The Cocaine Kids.* Reading, Mass.: Addison-Wesley, 1989.

Williams, Terry, and William Kornblum. *The Uptown Kids: Struggle and Hope in the Projects.* New York: Putnam, 1994.

————. *Growing Up Poor.* Lexington, Mass.: D. C. Heath/Lexington Books, 1985.

Wolfe, Tom. *The Electric Kool-Aid Acid Test.* New York: Bantam Books, 1983.

Zola, Irving Kenneth. *Missing Pieces: A Chronicle of Living with a Disability.* Philadelphia: Temple University Press, 1982.

Zuboff, Shoshanna. *In the Age of the Smart Machine: The Future of Work and Power.* New York: Basic Books, 1988.

Index

Contributors

ELIJAH ANDERSON, Professor of Sociology, University of Pennsylvania.

VICTOR AYALA, Associate Professor, Department of Counseling, New York Technical College, City University of New York.

VERNON BOGGS, (late) Professor of Sociology, York College, City University of New York.

CHARLES BOSK, Professor of Sociology, University of Pennsylvania.

KIRK ELIFSON, Professor of Sociology, Georgia State University.

DOUGLAS HARPER, Professor of Sociology, Duquesne University.

RUTH HOROWITZ, Professor of Sociology, University of Delaware.

WILLIAM KORNBLUM, Professor of Sociology, City University of New York, Graduate School and University Center.

ROBERT P. McNAMARA, Assistant Professor of Sociology, Furman University.

EDMUNDO MORALES, Associate Professor of Sociology, West Chester State University.

NANCY A. NAPLES, Assistant Professor of Sociology and Women's Studies, University of California, Irvine.

CAROL STACK, Professor of Education and Women's Studies, University of California, Berkeley.

CLAIRE STERK, Associate Professor of Anthropology, Emory University.

PEGGY SULLIVAN, President, Quality Process Consulting, New Orleans.

WILLIAM F. WHYTE, Professor Emeritus, New York State School of Industrial and Labor Relations, Cornell University.

TERRY WILLIAMS, Associate Professor of Sociology, New School for Social Research.

About the Editors

CAROLYN D. SMITH is a writer and editorial consultant specializing in educational materials in the social sciences. She is the author of *The Absentee American: Repatriates' Perspectives on America* (Praeger, 1991).

WILLIAM KORNBLUM is the author of *Blue Collar Community* (1976) and co-author (with Terry Williams) of *Growing Up Poor* (1985) and other titles. Kornblum and Smith have collaborated in the writing and development of textbooks on sociology and social problems and are co-editors of *The Healing Experience: Readings on the Social Context of Health Care* (1994).

ISBN 0-275-95416-1

90000>

EAN

9 780275 954161

HARDCOVER BAR CODE